Equal Rights From God

The Equalitarian Age

Betty C. Dudney

ISBN: 0692221573
ISBN 13: 9780692221570
Library of Congress Control Number: 2014915365
LCCN Imprint Name: Golden Rule Family Publ.
Nashville, Tennessee, 37215, USA
equality4peace@yahoo.com
phone: 1-615-926-0967

T0 THOSE WHO LOVE GOD
AS CREATOR, THE SPIRIT OF HOLY LOVE
AND
EQUALLY FOR THOSE WHO HAVE YET TO
KNOW
TO "LOVE ONE ANOTHER"

INTRODUCTION

Inequality breeds war, destruction, Injustices of all kinds. To turn from we need moral as well as legal Equal Rights, Equal Respect, a real concern for People's needs.

Inequality as a belief system justifies discrimination, taking advantage of others, allowing profits, or positions of power, to become like gods.

Some of the strongest in positions of power, manage at the top of the worlds economy because their income comes primarily from profits, while the majority of people work instead for wages, most of them for the lowest legally allowed, and many without the minimum wage!

Even one major health issue in a family, an economic downturn, or a loss of a job can spell disaster.

For most workers trying to build a retirement fund, or for the majority of investors, not in a knowing inner circle, there will be recurring cycles of stock shocks.

The few 0.1 of 1% at the top of the economic power ladder have many well-paid staffs of managers, lawyers, as well as political ties that keep them in control, even from most people knowing who they are, or what they are doing.

Yet when enough people become aware, and are willing to work together, they hold the power to make life better for all!

TABLE OF CONTENTS

WHY GO TO ROME?

January 12, 2015

U.S. Apostolic Nunciature
Archbishop Carlo Maria Vigano,

Thank You for your letter.

From your letter I see what once had to be pointed out to me too, that the first two stories in Genesis about creation, are very different stories of how our world was created. It is not possible to combine the two stories into one!

In the first story of the first chapter, both male and female God created last, after the plants and other animals and both were created in "the Image of God". This first chapter is called the Priestly or the Godly version.

In a second story that starts in the second chapter of Genesis, a whole different story with an opposite order of creation, the man being created before the animals, or the woman. It is known as a parable of a talking snake, and is still being used by some, to justify inequality and sexism.

There is a third story that is the same as the first and official Priestly story of Genesis 1:27, repeats "both male and female are created in the Image of God" and found in Genesis 5:1.

Such stories of creation were told at nightly campfires for unknown hundreds, even thousands of years, by tribes of patriarchal males, before being written down, long before paper was invented.

The sooner the Church comes out of it's present inequality of discriminating against the female half, the sooner our world can become a better place to live, by treating each other with equal respect, opportunity.

"Equality" can be confirmed from God's Holy Spirit, as the essence of the New Testament Covenant to "Love One Another".

We want, need The Church to lead the way, the way of God's equal morality for all, to flow out into our world.

May God's Peace be with You,

Betty C. Dudney

There is no professional writer here, for writing I have found 'does not a writer make'. So forgive me for the grammatical mistakes and please listen for this hearts intentions.

Have always loved to write and to read books even more. Remembering when I was about 16 doing a little poetry, and asking God if I could be a reporter and make my living writing? In my head I heard "You'll never make your living writing."

So I went into Nursing, later was trained in a Medical Laboratory to become a Medical Technologist, because I liked better working on the why's of Medicine, while my brother became a Doctor, what our large extended family thought we ought to be.

After a lab accident that affected my health making it impossible to work anymore at a decent paying job, have tried writing about my spiritual experiences, but God was right as usual, and writing has only cost me in more ways than just money.

Witnessing for "Equality" even more so. But God is Good and it has been equally rewarding in more ways than I could ever have imagined.

One of the letters saved written to Pope Benedict XVI.

November 12, 2010.

Your Holiness Pope Benedict XVI,

Have known from the beginning it would be difficult to communicate with you. Even if we are in conflict Love, with its Godly purpose is the best and primary reason to change some things for the better for all of us.

Our Inequality hurts us all especially the female half of God's Image.

What we do here, or fail to do, affects so many.

We are the example of morality that should be flowing first from The Church into the world to end discrimination. * 1

God is not just male, or female, but is a combination of both gender qualities.

"In Christ, there is no male or female." *2

Our Church must soon reflect this fact or we face the judgment to us both in the present, as well as in the eternal hereafter.

Inequality is hurting The Church and is negatively affecting our world. Every human being, scientifically, mentally, or even more importantly spiritually, is composed of both sexual components, only in degree.

We are much more alike than we are different! Would prefer to come to Rome for Your Blessing for our Golden Rule Family, as we are increasing in numbers, and feel time is of the essence for us, our Church, and for the world to end inequality. To establish "Equality" in terms of Equal Rights, Equal Respect, Equal Opportunity!

If you continue to refuse to give women the right to serve "In Christ" at the altar, on the grounds Jesus did not appoint any, then the same logic should be applied that neither were Italians, Poles, or Germans, only Jews, or those in the Middle East, were appointed by Jesus.

*1 Pastoral Constitution, Article 29+, Vatican II 1965 *2 Gal. 3:28

I had felt led by God to witness to Pope Benedict XVI after earlier attempts to reach Pope John Paul II.

Going to Rome the first time in 1985 with the hope to help end discrimination within "The Church", as one of the major places where morality should be flowing out into the world.

To end discrimination against race or sex...as not God's Will was first given to The Catholic Church at the World wide council of Bishops (called about once every hundred years) and specifically stated in the Councils Pastoral Constitution, Article 29+, Vatican II in 1965.

It would be ten years later before I would specifically hear the actual word of "Equality" during my own Spiritual "Rebirth"*. *Jesus spoke of in John 3:3-5; and in I Peter 1:23.

It had become obvious discriminations were going to be continued within The Church. At least it was obvious to God, but being raised a Protestant I had not even heard at that time of such Catholic Councils.

Most of the male only controllers within the Church have tried to ignore or make light of this discrimination after the untimely death of Pope John Paul I, the first elected Pope after the Vatican II Council ended.

Many hundreds of women religious had come to see him, to seek equality, as well as point out some known irregularities in the Vatican Bank, and he had promised he would look into them, sighting Isaiah's and Jesus feminine references of God.

All this happening just three days before his untimely, questionable death, after only 33 days in office.

Now almost 50 years later do we have another such Holy Pope as this first John Paul I was? Pray that he is, and pray for his personal protection.

Experience has taught me God wants to, and does work through human hands of good will, when we are willing!

During the seventeen years I was able to work in Medical Clinics and Hospitals I only had a little time or energy left to give much extra, with a family to help support and care for.

So did nothing like my hero's of those days who gave so much, such as Mother Teresa or Gandhi and many that are not well known.

As was Marshall Ganz the only son of one of our local Rabbi's, a studious young man in college with a scholarship to Harvard. One of many who would give away promising futures, in his last year of college, to help make it possible for all races to have the right to vote, to help end the many prejudices, inequalities of those times.

Have known of several, mostly young people, who with others, spent their summers in the South, working for civil rights, some would not return!

Many had felt called during the time of Martin Luther King, when they realized the importance of helping register first time minority voters, as well as doing sit-downs at lunch counters where those of color had not been able to eat before.

Some were beaten for it, many thrown in jail, a few even killed. Those killed included a few whites but were mostly aimed at the blacks who wanting a better life.

To be able to possibly awaken the conscience of others all of them had to agree beforehand to witness non-violently.

For a non-violent Loving determination for change that is good, is the most powerful weapon against anything that is negative. Even for those who were martyred, they live on, and did not die in vain.

This was and is the Southern part of America, where I am ancestrally from. I have much family here and still love to be.

Especially now that there has been so much progress to treat people as equal human beings, with equal rights, among most of the people.

It would raise the consciousness of many once it became the issue, forcing them to decide by the goodness in their hearts, to end the prejudice. For most people want to do the right thing.

The Civil Rights struggle for "Equality" continues, and has now expanded to Women's Rights.

It was not until 1921, long after slavery had ended, before the right to vote became legal for American women, where they no longer would be the legal property of males.

In some places of our world they still remain the property of first the father, than the husband, and if he passes, his brother!

Just the other day I heard of a young 12-year-old girl being sold by her father for $12.00. What kind of father would do that?

Was he like so many others on the verge of starving, who did it just to be able to keep her from starving too? Was it to feed the rest of his family for a short time more? Or did he not believe in the equal human value of a female?

Anyway you look at it the selling of a human being lowers the value of everyone's life, our freedoms, and each one's free will, lowering it to that of no more than cattle!

Of similar interest to me in the early 70's, was hearing about a farm workers movement in the center of California's long San Joaquin valley, a great farming area.

I had gone to High School there in Delano, at the same time as a beautiful young girl Helen, who later became the wife of Cesar Chavez. They would join with another energetic and very pretty young Delores Huerta, a life long worker for her people's rights, and with others who had been trying to form a local union.

Together they were able to establish the UFW, The United Farm Workers Union by sharing their finances and meager food of rice and beans, flour or corn tortillas, for years on end, and against all odds. They would strike against low wages for long hours under the desert Valley's hot deadly sun.

For many other miserable working conditions, such as a lack of toilet facilities, pesticide exposure and even for clean drinking water.

Twice they would end up marching on foot, all 465 miles to the State Capitol in Sacramento. It started and remained partly as a Religious Pilgrimage for their many needed and better work laws.

I wanted to march too but because of my own needs and final choice to keep my job, I didn't get the chance until the second time about a year after Cesar's death, in the middle 90's.

Both marches started with first only 50, and the second time with less than 100 willing to walk all the way from Delano.

Yet we finally reached Sacramento about a month later, by walking at least 12-15 miles a day. By then many 100's had heard of it, and even 1000's joined us in the last few days.

For me it had the health effect of turning up my immune system, to begin to start to work normally again.

During this second March, as we passed mostly farms, on the country roads, some of the workers would come out realizing what we were trying to do and some would join us, even a few more the next day.

As we walked by, most would at least wave, some offered food and others even a place to sleep that night.

A small truck with our sleeping bags followed behind. We slept in yards, as well as living rooms. Where we were met with such a positive response, increasing the closer to Sacramento we got and as more people joined us.

It took many years for farm workers to even be allowed to legally strike in the fields, for their families, their children's future, for a better life. Their union the UFW, continues to work hard for them.

In America, especially since the 1930's, it has been primarily the unions that have worked hardest for the workers rights.

People's unions as well as group networking for Equal Rights Worldwide, are needed now, as a needed balance from so much political as well as economic inequality.

Many things helped to end the war in Viet Nam, but surely public protest played a necessary part.

Peace vigils that friends began continue, as well as one war after another still goes on.

I had been feeling for a long time more called to witness against the discriminations within my own Church, specifically to the Pope as the Head of our largest group of Christians, of over a billion now in our world.

To also stop the justification of inequality for the pitiful low wages creating the huge profits for a few major stock owners, primarily those who own the majority voting control of the largest and the most powerful International Corporations. There are less than 300 of them, compared to 7 billion people, whose economy they control or greatly affect!

Our present cultural inequality, fueled by discrimination and inequality in the major religions gives them a moral free ride to squeeze ever more profits from the people's work and land.

To the point where half of the world's incomes are so low that as many as a third of the people are now trying to survive on as little as one meal a day. Wages for as little as $2-3 dollars a day.

Not an hour, a day! A slow starvation diet for millions!

Can you see a population control plan, in part by the use of starvation wages? With little concern for so many. Plus by the gradual increase in the costs of living it can eventually make work-like-slaves out of many of the rest of us too!

It is being done partly by the gradually tightening of the noose, of more work for less pay, enforced by a few top CEO's and some Department Heads richly rewarded by many millions in salary contracts, perks, and bonus, to see how much profit they can squeeze out of the workers!

Most everybody can understand why extra hard and extra dangerous jobs, those that require a lot of study, training, or skill, should be rewarded in a fair and just manner.

Or when people develop a special talent, create a new thing or serve the common good, they do deserve to be extra compensated for.

Yet tell me how can anyone's time, energy be worth thousands, even hundred's of thousands more money per day, than another persons time and efforts?

No way can such a difference be justified, except as legalized greed. This is an inequality that dates from age-old patriarchal traditions of lording it over workers.

This misuse of people's Time and Labor, of their energy and limited resources, the unfair power of money in control, instead of People's equal rights having at least an equal say.

One of us can do very little about it, but how many petitions, letters, or Unions of people would it take for not only a worldwide minimum wage, but also a cap for maximum wages, or maximum % of profits.

Excesses at a certain point should, could be used to provide for more equitable sharing of the profits that are made off the workers labor and efforts?

Used for equally needed low-income safety nets, for children in school that could stop the high illiteracy rate, of over 50% we now have, in our world. Those who need to learn to read and write or develop a skill, before being forced into the work place in slave like wages. Children who are now being put into the labor market at 5-6 years old!

If petitions, letters, and phone calls prove unsuccessful there are other legal, non-violent ways to change the present situation, but only when enough people have come to realize the need and priority, then are willing to become unselfish enough to commit to finding enough others to work with, to make it possible.

They would have God's Blessings, and would surely find the means, as they do have the power to make life better for themselves, as well as others.

But only when enough people can see how it is in their long time best interest, and the dangers we all face ahead, if we do not make the needed changes now.

Not only to save millions of lives but for a chance at a good life, for each according to their talent, interest, or ability, with an equal opportunity at least within reach.

Otherwise we will continue to sweep under the rug, so many without equal rights or a safety net and allow them to continue to be exploited? We then become the participants, along with the exploiters!

First find networks to work with, such as Golden Rule groups of different kinds, willing to work for the basic needs of the most needy, to chop at the root causes. Work with those who have a plan for a better fairer world.

When many can believe God is with the people's rights, they will surely see many ways to act before more damage has been done.

It is not just myself who have been given a vision from God, or what some believe to be their spiritual intuition.

There is a Spirit of Equity in our world now that most of us do recognize, speaking in several ways to many good people. We have seen some growing effects in the last 50 years.

Such as a progression from a patriarchal dictatorship of very few and powerful, to a more Equalitarian or Democratic rule of the people, when people realize they have the right and power to make a better life real.

MEN'S TRADITIONS

This is the letter I had given to the Swiss Guards at the entrance to The Papal suites in the Vatican, in hopes of reaching the desk of one of the Popes Secretaries who might pass it on to him:

"Men's ways, or traditions have evolved since primitive times, such as slavery, racism and sexism, and other forms of unfair inequality.

We now understand and can confirm by The Holy Spirit, at least those whose conscience are clean, that we are not to belittle or to enslave another human being.

The same is true for male and female relationships and equally applies to 90% of the people, who are trying to survive on so little of the world's wealth and resources. Our great and growing economic disparity, a gross imbalance of inequality, is not godly, or good for anyone.

It is a sad misuse of men's traditions of greed and power tripping, and not from a Holy or a sacred God of Love.

The true living God is "not a god of partiality", is "a God of Equity". Which Scriptures have pointed out, as well as Vatican II: to end discrimination, such as racism and sexism, within the Church as not the Will of God.* Pastoral Constitution Article 29+ Vatican II, in 1965."

April 6, 2011

This is my fifth day of praying and fasting in St. Peter's Square at the fountain below the Pope's windows, for an end to inequality and discrimination within our Church where our morality should be flowing.

Psalms 126 tells us to give thanks for all we have.

We can give thanks, if for nothing else for the very air we have to breath. And it also says: "Those who sow in tears, shall reap in joy"!

Such things happen in God's timing, not always in ours.

It is one of God's promises to give us hope in this life as well as the next.

In spite of my own share of tears I see my long life has also been blessed with much, and most of all with that great hope of eternal life.

How can we thank God enough for that hope?

With that hope it makes it easier to continue to give thanks when life seems more of a burden than worth going on.

It is faith in that great hope that makes it possible to overcome the suffering, and turn it towards the means to help us up another step onto a better ladder, even sometimes making it possible to find our heaven in this life, but mostly having it to look forward to.

If even our worse can be turned to good, then it is a reason to seek God's Hand, especially in times such as these.

Also turned to I Peter in the New Testament, Chapter 5.

For once at a mountain retreat, a Monk Priest had confirmed my habit of turning to pages within scriptures to try to fit a current need. Creating a picture in words, of what I would recognize I needed to know at that time!

Coincidence?

Well it must then confirm with the universal Golden Rule, for it is easy to take Scriptures out of context, a word that might only apply to other times or men's traditions.

This time I turned to where St. Peter speaks to the elders telling them to "Feed the flock freely, not for money, but with a willing mind. Not to be as Lord's over what is God's, but to be the better example'. *I Peter 5:2,3.

Then to the younger ones in I Peter 5:5 where he says: "all are to be subject to one another, wearing the clothing of humility, for God rejects and allows the proud to stumble, but gives grace to the humble".

Could I be here fasting and praying in this sackcloth and not feel humbled?

Strangely enough there is also a sense of being close to heaven, not in a physical present day situation but in a spiritual sense that is difficult to describe just sometimes a little sight, a feeling of the hope yet to be, so for now I must wait on God's Holy Spirit as Jesus says, to give me more direction.

May 23, 2011

For Pope Benedict XVI,

It always seems incredulous to go from such a miserable day to a Blessed Day, but that is what has happened to me on this day, even though it is beginning to rain again.

Had a chance to talk to a woman, also praying below your window, who seemed to understand what I was doing here in sackcloth with the cross on it that has the = sign as the cross bars, although we both earlier had only made a few attempts to communicate very deeply, more than just recognize each other as praying friends.

I have been seeing her at the fountain where I usually go for several hours a day to say my rosary's, while looking up at your window far above, often after first coming out of St. Peters to go to morning communion.

Even with her little bit of English and my poquito, or um poi Italian, we have finally managed to understand each other enough to know that about 3 years ago, she had a vision from God about The Church needing to accept women as equals. While I had been told by God's Holy Spirit the one word of "Equality", over forty years ago.

My first encounter 25 years before that, I was shown The Hand of God, at only 5 years old. I believe at so young an age to keep me from ever thinking it was from any of my own merits. Kind of like when Eli was called by God as a child. Many seem to be called by God in their early years and probably for the same reason.

I see this meeting with this other Witness as another confirmation for an end to inequality. "Equality" should come from the Church where God's morality should always be flowing!

I am hoping you do already know this woman, as she says she is in touch with one of your private Secretaries, a Monsignor, who is the same one I had received a response with his signature, to show you received a letter, I wrote to you from America, about a year ago.

Since coming here this time have not been sure what God has in mind, but here is this other witness who also feels called by God to witness for "Equality", within our Church.

It seems more than just a coincidence and I'm elated, for it is another sign to me that God is leading the way.

She says that you are in agreement, from her talks with your secretary, who arranged a room here at the Vatican for her, and asked her to just continue to pray each day. So it seems probable that God has led us here, to witness together now.

Raised as a Protestant, I learned much about Scriptures and even more since God led me into the Catholic Church, where I was confirmed in 1975.

Have learned to love The Church but could not stand the bad that I also saw in it, even tried to leave once by turning away and walking back towards where I lived then.

After less than a block away I felt God's Hand in mine, was not able to see it as I had at five years old, but felt it this time as well as God's greatest Power again, as it spun me around in my tracks, back towards the Church.

So there is no doubt in my mind God wants me to stay within the Church to help it be the best it can be. With males only in control, our Church is so unbalanced right now. It may be hard to even see the damage it is doing to our world.

As it gives a rationalization to the secular world and other beliefs, to continue their own discriminating towards the female half.

Just as bad if not more so, many people maybe over half of all people are being economically badly affected by this belief in inequality and the lack of Equity in the world's economy.

These practices of inequality in The Church are helping others to rationalize their inequality. Rationalize an economy of up to 90% of which is owned or controlled by less than 2%. Controlling our world's resources that God has created to be best used for all.

Our Church by continuing to practice discrimination makes void or hard for others to believe in, or to practice the good that is also preached.

In another letter I also told him how I had first came to Rome to witness about inequality in 1985, to see the then Pope, John Paul II, who did not do what God sent me there for, to end discrimination within The Church. He made it instead that much harder for women.

Instead at least for me, another kind of Miracle had happened. In my spare time I had been visiting different Church's in Rome, looking for evidence of Saints who had been miraculously preserved after death, and had found one who really looked fully preserved.

Only one who did still look perfect, and in a glass coffin, so I could see him up very close. Looking so real even with little hairs on his ears and a graying of the hair on his head. Yet, there was no way to be sure it was not just a wax reproduction.

This had been a Cardinal who had lived here in Rome some 500 years ago. A son of a prominent Prince from Sicily, he had given up his rich worldly life to become a servant within the Church!

When I heard he was going to be canonized at St. Peter's, I felt I had to go, and wanted to. While at the service I had been told to ask for one of the numerous miracles that are suppose to happen to some who go, as a witness to his Sainthood.

Usually one of healing, yet I had asked for what seemed like a simpler one for this new Saint, his Spiritual name being St. Giuseppe Maria Tomasi. It was just to see a Priest friend before I had to leave in about a week, going on to Jerusalem in the Holy Land, where Jesus had lived.

The Priest had been in Rome for about a year on a Sabbatical leave, but I had no idea where he would be staying.

Thought I had seen him not long before as he walked across St. Peter's Plaza with another Priest, but did not want to run after him!

Surely my miracle would be that we would just meet on the way out of this special Mass. Yet would I have believed it had really been a miracle, if it had happened that way, I doubt it?

Actually on my way home, had concluded what I had seen must just have been a wax representation.

Feeling very tired and let down, as the bus wound on to the very edge of Rome and just looking forward to taking a nap in my little room, with a shared kitchen and bath, the only affordable one I had found, for the three months here in Rome.

After only about 15 min. of lying down, I suddenly was wide-awake with a strong feeling I should get up and go to see the beach. This would be at least an hour's trip away by train even after I got back into Rome's main train station!

I had already seen most of the city from going back and forth to the Vatican, but had not gone to the beach to see the Mediterranean Sea.

Not really having enough extra money to do this either, but the urging was strong and so I went.

First taking a bus back into town, where I had just come from, and getting on about an hour's train ride to the beach.

As the train arrived I could see to walk straight down to the water, only a short distance away and then turning to my right started walking along the waters edge.

A little bridge crossed a small stream that ran into the sea and as I got on top of it, here was this Priest I had asked St. Giuseppe to see! Right there in front of me, walking with a Priest friend.

We both were a little stunned as I tried to explain, as best I could in the moment we took to say hello, and then trying not to completely block the traffic going both ways, so others could pass, then on down the path we both went, in our opposite directions until I saw another path that led back to the train.

Decided to take it and go back to Rome for I had now had my Miracle. Yet when I got back on the train, here they were again, already sitting, having gotten on the stop before by going in the opposite direction, and going where I had first come down to the seashore.

So I was even able to explain a little more in detail how my seeing him there had happened. The other

Priest didn't seem too sure, to believe it or not, but the two of us knew. Didn't want to cause him any more possible trouble by reporting this happening to any of the Church authorities so I didn't.

GOD OUR MOTHER AS WELL AS FATHER

To see God as just a male, is Idolatry creating a false image of God, keeping us in a state of inequality; instead of learning to equally cooperate with each other.

This past week's audience with Pope Benedict XVI went best, so far as I did managed to get the prayer of "Equality" to one of his aides as they passed where I was standing.

Standing along with thousand's of others for hours since early in the morning, to be as close as possible as he travels around the crowds and up to the middle of the platform in front of St. Peter's Basilica, this huge Church that looks out over the Vatican and the surrounding columns of a gigantic St. Peter's Plaza.

They come here from all over, many on vacation for the Popes message and weekly Blessing.

"EQUALITY"

FOR EQUAL HUMAN RIGHTS
ESPECIALLY WITHIN THE CHURCH
FROM WHERE GOD'S MORALITY FLOWS,
LORD HEAR OUR PRAYER

FOR EQUAL HUMAN RESPECT
THE BALANCING OF UNBALANCENESS
FROM DISCRIMINATION AND PREJUDICE
OH LORD HEAR OUR PRAYER

FOR EQUAL HUMAN CONCERN
TO END THE PRESENT INEQUALITY
A WAY TO BRING BACK MANY TO GOD
LORD HEAR OUR PRAYER

FOR MUTUAL OPPORTUNTY
THE HOLY SPIRIT SPOKE IN VATICAN II
SPEAKS NOW TO ALL GOOD HEARTS
OH LORD HEAR OUR PRAYER.

This is the prayer I gave to Pope John Paul II, the first time I witnessed here before going on to Israel; for what I thought God wanted me to go there to do, a Peace Scroll, as an all out war seemed near.

Pope John Paul II did stop in front of me in the third month, two weeks before I had to leave, but I was so surprised for he rarely seemed to stop that I could only hand him the above poem!

On the very last Wednesday I could go to the audience I promised God if he would stop him one more time, I would overcome my shyness to speak to him of our Church's need for "Equality", and would you believe it, he did! But wouldn't you know it, a beautiful rich young looking woman with many jewels, came pushing her way through and crowded in beside me.

His response to me then, was just to have one of his aides hand me a prayer card of a young Jesus, like as a 2-3 year old child, without any clothes!!!

A third leg needed to preach? Good Lord, how will I get though to him now?

At least I am not feeling as shy about speaking!

And about this time wrote:

IF JESUS CAME BACK AS A WOMAN!

IF JESUS CAME BACK AS A WOMAN
WHERE WOULD SHE GO TO PREACH?
CERTAINLY NOT TO THE MOTHER CHURCH
FOR THAT IS CLAIMED BY MALES
FOR MALES ONLY!

PERHAPS TO A CONVENT
INSIDE CLOSED DOORS BE HEARD
THE SAME CLOSED DOORS OF THE TEMPLE
2000 YEARS AGO
WHERE WOMEN WAITED IN THE OUTER COURT
AS PROPERTY

NO WONDER OUR WORLD IS STILL IN CHOAS
WHEN ONLY HALF OF THE WHOLE
PRESUMES TO RULE OVER THE OTHER HALF!

Thought I wrote another verse but maybe not, as can't find any more.

The first month, I stayed In Jerusalem, a pilgrimage to my European ancestral roots as a Huguenot Christian, within a 16th Century like French Convent, right on the Via Del Rosa, or Way of The Cross, where Jesus had last walked, in the Arab or poorer section of the high walled Old City.

On the first night the taxi, from the plane at Tel Aviv, left me off at the Donkey Gate as the streets inside the walled Old City are two narrow for cars. I didn't know it then but the Convent was only a few blocks away, from where I was let off with a suitcase and backpack, about 10 at night.

Could only see a few poorly dressed young men standing near the wall. As they began to gather around me, I began to fear.

Would you believe they only came to see if they could help, and when I gave them the address they insisted on carrying everything. Even refusing money for helping me when we got there!

They are like so many of the young people, in most places I've been, who have such a precious sweet willingness to be helpful, even to strangers.

Surely not many of them feel very safe with their world as it is, more so now but even then, it must have been scary for those living there.

The Old City, at least at that time was divided into three sections of the three religious offshoots, of Abraham's descendents. Both Jews and Muslims had about an equal amount of living, and business sections, with a smaller Christian section in between of mostly religious buildings.

Outside the walls of the Old City of Jerusalem, the city extends into much larger Jewish and Muslim areas, with only a few Christian areas found outside the giant blocks that make up the thick, several story high walls of the majestic Old City, brightly lit both day or night.

Bethlehem the little city of Jesus birth, is only two miles away and almost completely Arab, as are most of the smaller towns.

This now state of Israel given after World War II by the League of Nations, as a homeland for the Jewish people, is also the homeland of many Muslims, who had called it Palestine for Centuries.

Jews, Muslims, and Christians, all have reason to think of it as their special Holy Land too.

Three separate but related beliefs, hopefully soon to learn to be tolerant of each other, or they will continue to be a most dangerous threat, to each other and for worldwide peace.

Except for facing the Mediterranean Sea this land is surrounded by Lebanon, Jordan as well as Egypt.

All the way to Tiberius on the Sea of Galilee to the mountains of Cana, and Nazareth, where Jesus was known to be from, still seemed in 1986, to be mostly Arabs.

Now I have heard there are many more highly fortified Jewish settlements in or nearby those towns, than there were then, in early 1986.

A friend I soon met helped me with a Peace Scroll and we went to several Peace marches composed of hundreds, right to the Prime Ministers House.

The people, by nature most want peace, but some are willing to gamble for what they see as gain. Yet everyone loses in the violence and destructiveness of war, inside, as well as in others.

Without mutual forgiveness and reparation now, it will continue to boil.

International politics created it, and should have already intervened to settle it!

After a month's stay in Jerusalem on the Convent sleeping porch, that overlooking the third station of the Via Del Rosa, I found a little one room inner court apartment, right across the alley from the Armenian Monastery, with a old ancient great Library.

Here I would find my real reason for coming here, the definition of "ABBA", in the language Jesus used, later translated in Biblical versions as only "Father".

Going to the land where Jesus lived and taught, allowed me to understand a lot more about my relationship with God, especially after learning with more certainty that God is our Mother, as well as Father.

The Librarian at the Monastery Library helped me to see for myself the ancient documented evidences that "ABBA" does not mean just the Father but also includes the Mother as well.

One of the original clues for me had been the Gospels of Jesus where "ABBA" usually translated as "Father" had not been translated, as in the passage of Mark 14:36.

This is one of the few Biblical places where the word "ABBA", the word Jesus used for God, was kept in His original language. To give the original word Jesus used for God as both the Mother and the Father or our "Heavenly Parent".

The combining of the two letters "AB" for Father and "BA" for Mother, to form the parent word of "ABBA", to mean our Heavenly Spiritual Parent.

When you stop and think about it, a Father is only half of the Perfect Parent. God has the qualities of a Mother too.

The first, as well as the third Creation story* in Genesis tells us. We are both made in the Image of God, male and female. *

*Genesis chapter1: 27; and chapter 5:1

What a relief to find this evidence that God is not just a 'Male Only' God. This has made a difference in my feelings for others both male and female, as well as towards God, in a fuller, more loving way.

Even though I had a very loving and good human Dad, as well as a good Mom and can't image what my relationship with others would be like if I hadn't.

Or if I had ever really accepted that God was male only, but it never seemed just right to me.

Maybe it would depend on what kind of parents or caretakers one has had, but it sure would make it very difficult to even want to know such a one sided God, especially if there had not been a good male parental relationship while growing up.

For some males not all for sure, but for some, it also seems to give them a false sense of superiority or entitlement, a Lordship from just their being male.

Have also noticed females often seem to have a sense of inferiority, or think more highly of males than females! It is bound to have caused relational problems towards each other, for many.

Realizing God as our Heavenly Parent, including the best traits of both Mother as well as Father, can't help but give us better examples, make a difference in how we even subconsciously as well as consciously, treat each other.

While living in the Old City of Jerusalem, one of my Jewish neighbors went out of his way to be helpful even encouraging me to become a Jewish citizen.

Yet some or his reasons were disturbing to me, as he claimed his religious party, who are still very much in power there, believe they have "The Messiah" with even supernatural flesh, guiding their leaders as an anointed one from God, yet it was not to be publically acknowledged?

This "Messiah" he said, had performed supernatural cures, or on at least one top Religious Rabbi, he knew and had in other ways convinced those in power by such things as "you could put your hand into his side and have it come out without feeling anything substantial, or your hand would not have any blood on it".

This seemed to me like a possible hypnotic suggestion, possibly a magicians trick, since I was sure this could not be the return of Jesus, who said He would come back from the heavens, to be seen by and for all.

This "Messiah's" purpose seems only in convincing them they should drive their ancestral cousins the

Arabs out of what has been the land, both have lived on for centuries? Causing much trouble. Contrary to what most of the Jewish and Arab people I met there wanted, certainly no more war.

Actually for many hundreds of years a relative few Jewish people, have always lived here in this land, among many of their Arab "brothers" and have been able to live in peace together.

If what he told me is true, this sounded more like what Christians know of as an Antichrist, who could very well have some supernatural powers but not from the God who sent Jesus, or not from a Creator God of All people.

Except my Jewish neighbor there, didn't believe in Jesus, had not read Christian Prophecy, or the Gospels. So he has no reason to think this is not their Messiah if that is what his Religious leaders say!

My best reasoning, for thinking this is most likely a dangerous counterfeit, leading them to ever more destruction, is that when Jesus or The Messiah returns, Christian prophecy says he will not come in secret, or to favor just one race, but to all and for all, and for all to see, for all to be judged.

There is also an allotted time for evil to pass before Jesus returns, according to Revelations Chapters 12 & 13, in the last book of the Bible.

The allotted time could be as many as five to six hundred more years from now, if the combined allotted times is doubled to include both the times of "The Dragon and The Beast". Counted from the times of the birth of Jesus, or the birth of the Church, or?

Where a prophetic day is know as a year in time.

True the times can and are said to be shortened to allow some believers still to be left, but since it has already been 2000 years since the prophecy was given, is doubtful it would be shortened by most of the 500+ years left of prophetic time, since there are still so many believers who are still here.

While It is possibly to see how many could fall away from a belief in Jesus as The Messiah, or even in God as an intelligent being, in a couple hundred years from now, but for right now there are at least many millions, maybe more who still believe in God, and the time was to be shorten so that at least some would still be here when Jesus does return.

There are also other signs that are supposed to happen before Jesus returns. Such as the Temple being rebuilt, with the sacrifices of animals and other such signs.

Some could be said to have already happened, or are in the process but there are more that will most likely take at least a few more generations, such as the death of the oceans.

If we do not make an abrupt turn to Equal Concern, to come out of our greed and inequality the oceans and water supplies will be damaged, at an even faster rate.

It must be up to us, those now here, to try to do our best to prevent the worse from happening we can now see we are headed for.

That is the primary reason Prophecy is given, to turn us towards a better direction, to warn us to make the needed changes, to turn the worse to being better for all. We have that power now, in our hands to do, but for how much longer?

HUMMINGBIRDS AND GODS

This morning sitting behind the screen of my back door, watching a few house sparrows eating bread crumbs, a sliver of a silver Hummingbird noticed hovering in midair, less than a foot away from my face, as if to say thank you for feeding them, as it click, click, clicked away, and then flew to a favored honeysuckle flower nearby.

Such little ones must see me like a good god, among other gods who care less, just as I can only see my God in such a limited way.

Physical living beings are each unique in what they see about their world, or can perceive God to be!

For me there have been few doubts about there being an Intelligent Living and Loving God, because of seeing literally the Hand of God on my fifth birthday and the feeling of God's supernatural Power and Love, then and many times in my life, so obviously greater than any other reality ever felt or seen.

It would be twenty-five years later in my early thirties, before I would be given another such sign and only when finally, I was fully willing to allow God's Holy Spirit into my heart, mind, soul, would I be able to recognize when God's Holy Spirit wanted to guide me.

All Spiritual guidance, thoughts from your own mind, what you read or given to you from others, should first be confirmed by the Universal Golden Rule, that is found naturally in loving hearts and in most world beliefs!

To treat others fair, as you would most like to be treated, even your enemies, is the kind of a Holy Love Jesus was talking about, when He said: This is the what the Laws and the Prophets are all about. *Matthew 5:44; 7:12; 22:39; Luke 6:27

Moses testified he saw God's Hand, 4000 years ago, who gave him the Ten Commandments for his people.

A couple thousand years later the prophet Daniel interpreted God's "Finger" writing, on the wall of the King's Banquet Hall, it had also been seen by many of those dining with the King.

Over 200 times I have found the mention of "God's Hand" in Biblical Scriptures, usually as a symbolic sign of God acting in our world, but sometimes, like in my case as a 5 year old child, literally seen, but only to be literally felt once more, in my long lifetime.

The second time so many years later, felt the Power of God's Hand actually in my hand, and it happened about a half block after I had decided to walk away from The Church and didn't want to go there anymore, for what seemed to me at the time as several valid reasons.

Yet God's Hand spun me back around towards "The Church" making me realize this is where I was to go with the message of God's "Equality", to help to end the people's inequality and discrimination there, as where it was most needed.

"Equality" or Equal Rights being the essence of the Universal Golden Rule found within the hearts of good people, of treating others with an equal fairness, the way you would best like to be treated.

It is also found within the created hearts of most developed, loving kind, undamaged or developed minds of life forms.

The doing of good, instead of evil, even to our enemies, makes it possible to create friendships, to lesson the tensions and other misunderstandings of life, to not increase the mistrust of others that can end so badly.

It makes it possible to evolve to higher realms of being, instead of destructive behavior that hurts both spirit and soul.

Yet some humans are either born or damaged in some way, physically, emotionally, in the area of their brain or "heart" that normally by nature gives them the ability to feel for, or care about others.

With well developed minds otherwise, they would learn about their lack of feelings for others maybe early in life and become aware of their lack of not caring but would tend to hide that lack of concern.

They would justify pretending to care as one of their most effective ways to be able to get what they want, or their needs met.

This is beyond just a selfish immaturity most of us grow out of and hopefully it is a rare inability not to be able to have feelings or real concern for others.

For without such feelings they would find it easy to use cunning, sneaky, even cruel ways, or as a last resort, violence to gain positions of power over others, in the home, at work, or in any other kind of organization, civil, or political, and even in religious positions.

Their pleasure of life, other than for food or sex, would come primarily by being in control of others to doing their will, and the misuse of others for their own, more important to them, selfish needs.

Most of us do limit to some degree, our feelings for those we don't see as being very much like us, especially those of different races and those not culturally or religiously raised in a similar way. We can also be mistrustful or fearful of others just because of differences.

Those unable to be concerned for others, who have little or no compassion or empathy, would see those smaller or those under them, even as possible prey!

In many loving caring hearts of animals, as well as in most humans, you find evidence of a concern for others, even at their own expense. But not in the forms of life that are just conditioned for self preservation, or not in those whose beliefs have taught them treating others unequally or unfairly is alright.

For some, if it is for making money or profits, then it becomes possible to justify a separate morality, also for those we see as in a different status, belief system, or as an enemy.

People can also be stirred up with fears and passions of revenge, for wrongs blamed rightly or wrongly on others, to the point of wanting to go to war, usually with those who belong to a different racial, religious, or culture group.

We have a long patriarchal history of one war after another, usually by males in control. Males having more aggressive male hormones, while females with less aggressive male hormones are more likely to look for more cooperative ways that would tend to prevent wars.

This is one of the reasons why we need Equal Rights, opportunity, for political, and religious balance, in both our legal as well as moral leaders.

Somewhere around 10,000 to 5000 years BC, in the previous Matriarchal age, before our present 5000 year old Patriarchal Age, Archeologist have now found evidence it was a much more peaceful time, more concerned with preserving the home and life in general when primarily the female half ruled for about 5000 years.

Partly evidenced by female gods, and only a few weapons used for hunting found, nothing like those later used primarily for war, when males began to dominate the cultures about 5000 years ago.

To help Co-Create our own Equalitarian Age of Equal Concern, Equal Rights, it helps to know that God is our Mother as well as Father, or of the "Equality" of God.

Much of our learning is on a subconscious level, much of the subconscious "knowing' imprinted before the age of 5. Only gradually have many humans evolved to increase their conscious awareness, or to focus much time on the higher God part of our brains, quiet different from the bottom or stem part, that is concerned primarily with our self-interests, such as eating, sex, and being personally in control, or getting our share!

Some can become very adept at hiding such a lack of feelings. Others may have been indoctrinated since birth of their superiority, because of their birth or family line.

This explains a lot of the last 5000 years of patriarchal oppression, enforced ultimately by those who were born into or have climbed, in a morality of inequality, to the top of the political, economic, and even religious power pyramids, by whatever means possible.

Pyramids of political power that look now like most of our Corporate Institutions.

It seems probably that some of the most powerful, who usually keep well behind the public scenes, but who also have the pull of so many strings, have little or no feelings or any great concern for the masses of people.

Seeing war, or starvation, as forms of population control, even to encouraging political leaders into one war after another, to be able to reap the great profits of high paying contracts for a great variety of war machines, both ground and air, contracted out to the larger corporations, becoming more and more lethal, and endangering most of our earth!

Down through the ages some of the Emperors, Cesar's, Kings, even a few Queens, have shown little conscience in using or misusing people to increase their own power, gain, or fortunes.

Instead of seeking mutual cooperation or negotiated solution's, in the better Golden Rule way, they have used wars that resulted in many deaths; emotional and mental, as well as much physical destruction.

The violence of wars are against the best or higher interest of all, even those few who end up profiting materially will be harmed sooner or later from the results of these negative actions.

We can expect this to continue until we are able to insure more legal as well as other kinds of safeguards against a very small minority who have taking so much advantage of millions, even billions of people.

To survive more disasters, even nuclear wars we must also find ways to stop misusing, destroying our planet.

I believe those who want safeguards from our present day man made disasters are way in the majority.

Yet many may be hesitant, to rock their own shaky economic boat, since most of us, except for the very rich and elite, are deliberately kept just one or two paychecks from financial disaster. Where even a lifetime of savings can be wiped out by sudden, and ever so often cyclic economic changes, by a disfavor of higher ups, or for that matter even by many serious health concerns, or hospital visits.

Drastic changes are constantly happening and are ever at our door, too often held over our heads, much like a hostage ransom, or threats.

These will remain in one form or another, and will get even worse, if enough of us fail to join with enough others, to do what we can for the rights of all, at this critical time in our world history.

It is possible when just a few who have had enough, come together and find ways to make needed changes. Often when a few will make the first move, others will join with them.

Once I know from just the beating of pots and pans with spoons and walking through neighborhood streets, a determined four were able to rally hundreds of people for support of a local community need, long neglected but being solved in one day. When hundreds of citizens showed up, respectfully, and non-violently, at a city council meeting, the council did act in their favor!

What is it going to take for many worldwide needs? Easy to feel it is too late, even to start, but it may be that it is just now possible to act with success!

Small golden rule groups of 10-12 close friends or family can network with larger groups to know where and how best to do something.

By choosing to do nothing we will eventually have to say, as was said after the Holocaust of World War II:

"I heard what they did to others but I thought I would be safe, if I just minded my own business. Then when they came for others nearby we were still afraid to do anything. By the time they came for us there was nothing left to do".

This world we live in is now everybody's business, it is our livelihood, our only home as long as we are here!

God warned the Israelites long ago, when they first considered having a King as they saw others have, that to have such Rulers, instead of Just Judges they did have, would cost them much, the best of their children and economic first fruits, a lot of their freedoms.

History tells us most Dictatorships or Kings have not been good for most of the people.

Wars kill off so many of the young, does untold damage to the minds and bodies left on both sides, as well as destroy needed resources, personal property, polluting the land and seas.

Insensitive or greedy leaders, with only pretend feelings or conscience, will tend to ignore warnings, even in leading us to "repeat the past" with ever more disastrous, now even nuclear weapons that can very negatively affect life on this planet for many hundreds of years to come.

Prophets have been warning of the dangers of a World War III for a long time. We have barely managed to avoid it several times in the past 50 years and we are still on the brink of a great disaster.

It is going to take many small groups working with larger groups to be able to prevent the worse from happening, at the least to mitigate the dangers. Our free will choice most of us must make, one way or the other, for we are the only ones here now, who are responsible for what we do, or fail to do, in our times.

The best way for those who can accept it, is to start first, daily with yourself, asking a Loving God into your heart, so you will know best what to do?

Being open to a Godly Intelligence within a loving heart is going to make it possible to more clearly see, know more than our limited physical minds can know, and guided more to the "Fullness of Truth" of John 14:26.

The fullness of Truth promised to those who love God and will Love One Another! A Godly kind of Love that extends even for your enemies* as the only way to make them friends instead of enemies! *Matthew 5:43,44; Luke 6:35

Small groups of like-minded friends working with each other for a better world have made a great difference and can again.

Yes We Can, "Si Se Puede!", Yes We Can, The Battle Cry of Delores Huerta we need now in Our Hearts!

There is plenty on this earth for all to have enough food, housing, education and training skills, but not if we continue to allow a few behind the scenes, hardened in inequality, to control most of our economy and our worlds resources, and instigating world conflicts.

It has been ignoring what is best for most people, with the power money buys, even violence, that has been used by some as their way of controlling, and misusing others.

Any chance we have to turn the tide must be done primarily by non-violent efforts to avoid falling into their mindset of violence to force others, to do their more selfish will.

The Power of Non-violence within the many is stronger than the physical might of the few, for it carries the Power of a Loving Creator within.

Each of us can join with others to create networks with those you know or believe are interested in a better life, not only for themselves, but equally for all people. There will be opposition, for the struggle is for our souls or spirits, as well as for our life work!

Having morals against the hurting of others is to some considered a weakness. "Might makes what is right" seems right, to those who are only centered in the self. Yet the human spirit, would be in grave danger of being lost if we knowingly support the inequality, that keeps at the least a third, of our world's population on a near starvation diet, with so many other injustices.

THE EARTH IN MINIATURE

"The Earth In Miniature" was given to me by one of many 'Earth Angels' I've met along the way.

Written just a few years after the turn of this Century by an anonymous Columbian Professor, from where she said she too had come from, and just "happened" to be in Rome and across the hall, in the Y. the most reasonable and centrally located room I had found in Rome this time.

The Professor had reduced the population of the earth to the size of a small village of exactly 100 people.

This village would have 57 Asians, 21 Europeans, 8 Africans, and 14 persons from the Western Hemisphere!

52 would be female, 48 would be male.

70 would be non-white; the other 30 would be white, or Caucasian.

Only 30 would be Christians, 70 would not be Christians.

89 would be Heterosexual, 11 would be Homosexual.

In this village of 100 humans, less than 5, all males would own or have control of most of the Villages resources. They would be from, or have strong ties to the 14 North Americans.

Of the total 100 people in the Village 80 would live in sub human conditions, that is 80% of all people! 70 would not be able to read!

(Only in the last 15 years has a dent in that number been made. Thanks primarily to the U.N.'s Children's School efforts.)

50 or one half would be suffering from malnutrition, with 1 person on the verge of starvation.

One person out of those 100 would actual starve each day!

One would be pregnant and another would give birth to a child.

Only one of the hundred would be educated in a university!

By understanding and facing these facts perhaps we will want to educate, or share them with others.

Can this be fully comprehended without some measure of moral concern, action, for the well being of the whole in this village we all call our planet?

Along with this report came a colored picture of our earth, as seen from the space ship, without borders!

At least one classroom in every school should have such a display.

He would also say this:

"Yes, to reflect more deeply, if you have risen this morning with good health, have enough to eat, and no disease that is in the process of destroying your body, than you are much more fortunate than many who will not be able to survive very much longer."

"Even more, if you are not one of those who are caught up in an actual war, or in a violent conflict, be in jail or have the agony of being tortured, or the pain of slow starvation. If you have escaped all this, than you are much safer than the majority of the people in our world".

"If you have food in a refrigerator, clothes in a closet, a ceiling over your head and a place where you can sleep tonight, you are richer than most of the people in your world. You are also one of the fortunate ones if you can read this."

So work today as if you don't need the money. Yes even as if you have been really hurt like most of us.

Dance now, as if nobody will be seeing you. Sing now as if nobody is listening to you!" And Thank You Professor, for sharing that with us.

My addition: If you really want to know what it is to dance and sing in the most, best possible way, than you must help to see that all those in our world village, have enough to eat and a place to sleep.

This seems a part of all of our responsibilities. In some way to do what we can, but the desire must be first found in your heart.

One of the more compelling reasons may be because you see this inequality as a grave danger and disadvantage to yourself, as well as to others.

There are many unknown dangers and pressing needs to make this a number one priority today, every day now, until equal opportunity exist for most, if not for all of us?

It starts in our relationships with each other.

Treating each other with the universally known (in the heart of all good people) Golden Rule, or equal fairness.

For an inner Peace, more precious and lasting in our souls or spirit than all the hard cold physical gold we might think we could otherwise accumulate, only to find we will lose it all when God does call for each ones last breath. For we all live our lives only a breath away from that call.

I believe the best possible message from a God of All, is summed up in "LOVE ONE ANOTHER", to care for one another, as equally fair as possible.

Not for God's sake, for that source of Creation needs nothing, but for our own sake! This is by far the better, kinder, and safer way to live.

For the past 5000 years our history has been written, interpreted, and sometimes misinterpreted where more competitive, more aggressive males were able to gain the reigns of controls, in the home, in our workplaces, religions, and even in our governments.

So in our for sure known historical times, about 10,000 years ago, since cavemen times, of humans trying to live together in different ways, in different places, with different resources, we now have a need for the survival of the whole planet, to come out of our most violent ways, especially out from long nuclear warfare.

We even have the opportunity, as well as the need to come into the Equalitarian age, an age of Equal Rights, Equal Respect, Equal Opportunity.

An opportunity and a need to have a concern for not only those who are like us, but also for those who are not, in such a way that our rights are not intruding on others, or visa versa.

Living in such an unequal world as we have had, will take some conscious efforts at balancing and creating "Equality" in our relationships, to heal first ourselves if we need healing, and then to share that healing.

It makes sense to do so because any of us can find ourselves in some kind of minority if we are not already aware of some, and have or will eventually have a need to rely on other's equal respect, to be able to live in the best possible world.

Much of our past inequalities have been allowed to continue because of so many Patriarchal Hierarchal power systems we all live under. Plus natural fears of those who are different and how their ways might affect us negatively.

Such fears and insecurities, as well as these Patriarchal unequal inequalities are our primarily dangers to our individual and world safety now.

A safer world will require us to try to be more sensitive, intuitive, and tolerant to where others are, putting daily into practice our universally known Golden Rule.

On another mental and emotional level is the bringing to a conscious awareness the violence and dealing with the amount of force that has been used in the past to continue the unfair traditions, customs in religious, economic, and political systems.

These have been going on for so long, many of us are conditioned to accept it, and rationalize or feel we do not have the ability or energy to change it for the better?

Yet a non-violent revolution, to treat others more fairly has been going on for centuries.

The quest for a more Loving and Peaceful living with others, while in this life, is found in all cultures such as far back in the times of The Buddha, there have been many advanced and Revered Teachers we know, in many cultures and times.

In the teachings of Jesus, in one of the most male dominated times of history, His "Equality" of having women disciples as well as men, even though they were not allowed then to go into the main Temple or even Synagogues or Preach in public, was significant even if it was later downplayed.

One of the first deeds Jesus did after his death and resurrection was to send Mary Magdalene as his Apostle to the other Apostles, to announce the "Good News", of the Resurrection of Jesus from death into eternal life!

To me, Jesus is the closest to being like God that we have had in human flesh, the faith and culture I was raised in, since my Mother's womb.

Knowing the Jesus way as being a way of Holy Love.

There is one Universal "Way" of Holy Love, or of Spiritual growth, that can be found within both the Eastern as well as Western beliefs, and is expressed as living within The Golden Rule as a Holy Way of love, not just for yourself, but equally for others.

That Golden Rule can be found naturally within loving hearts, no matter whether they belong to a specific faith, or belief, even whether one has a belief in a Spiritual God! We all tend to adopt some kind of a god, even if it is just in our self, position, or money.

To commit to a way of equally caring for one another, is the way to have the best kind of Peace in our world. As we then will also have more physical security knowing people have their basic needs for life, and rights respected.

How can we justify just a few hundred, mostly males, having the right to take from Billions of men, women, children, so much more than their share, not only in terms of economic wealth, but claiming most of our worlds future resources, that is our power too?

How can only a small minority have the right to prevent the many from becoming the best each has the talent and interest to be?

If you know in your heart the answer is No! Then isn't it time to stop this present inequality?

Stopping wars and more nuclear disasters might seem to be a higher priority, yet don't they go hand in hand?

It will take the power of many to insist on fairer ways, to create a better world and do it in the most positive way for all. What are some of the ways that this could be done in a non-violently way?

Many Human Right groups working together from a local to an International level, for decent living wages as well as Equal Rights are needed. This is what could make it possible.

There are many human right groups now, who need more people willing to help to network with them and with each other, find at least one you can trust and can believe in to work with.

The first group we tried, we called it the Golden Rule Family, as a legal non-profit group, but it does not have to be such a legal or even a formal group. Best it seemed to us at the time of not more than 10-12, members with the intentions of when it became larger, one or two would break off to form another such group.

This is a way to grow and still be small enough to know and be able to work well with others.

It also encourages each one to form as many as 12 other small groups, with as few as two, of like-minded friends or co-workers working together.

That way groups form a network and yet work separate as where needed. Keeping in touch or to coordinate at times towards mutual goals, would only take a few members networking with other local, regional and International Groups, to keep each other informed when and where need be.

Contact can be kept with individual groups, while your primary efforts may be wherever each one feels they have the most to offer and feels best working in that area, be it local, national, or world wide.

This seems one of the best ways for such groups to not only sustain interest, but to accomplish much, even when necessary doing possible fundraising for agreed on goals, if and only when it cannot be done voluntarily.

As there should never be member dues, for the poorest of the poor should feel welcome to participate, without having to take needed funds away from their basic needs.

May take donations offered from those who have extra, but no money pressure for members helps build trust.

If there is a need of funds for a project, could offer such practical things as reasonably priced T-Shirts, possibly a design or logo, or other usable items at a reasonable cost. The majority would have to vote for any special event, for any specific needs.

One way too would be to share this message, as a $1.Amazon.com E-book with those you may want to build a Golden Rule group with.

Any profits made would go for making books or sites more available. A recent site now working for your suggestions or imputes.

www.worldwidehumanrights.org

IDOLATRY

SOME ARE TEMPTED DAILY TO MAKE GODS OUT OF THEIR PROFITS, ALLOWING EVIL AND INEQUALITY TO PROSPER WHILE THE YOUNGER, IN AGE OR KNOWLEDGE, SEEM TO SUFFER THE MOST!

IT IS ONLY WHEN WE COMMIT OURSELVES TO FOLLOW THE PERFECT HOLY LOVE, WITH ALL OF OUR HEART, MIND, AND SOUL CAN WE EXPECT TO HAVE THE BEST POSSIBLE GUIDANCE AND NOT BE CONTROLLED OR LED BY FALSE GODS OF IDOLATRY

NEGATIVE NATURE OF EVIL

My God does not have a negative nature, is not the cause of evil. I once thought that, because there seemed so many negative things that were attributed to God, before I realized even for inspired Prophets, all people's perceptions of God are limited to their space and living in their time.

Earlier perceptions were also limited primarily to the protection of the individual self, as in the family or extended family, as a race, nation, or belief system.

We have been evolving into the understanding, if not always the practice of The Golden Rule, as a

Universal belief standard, found in the hearts of most people, and we are at our best, when we put it into practice for the benefit of All, by cooperating and working with each other, rather than previous endless competitive conflicts ending in wars between nations, race and belief systems.

For good reasons the Creator of All is equally concerned with all, as a Heavenly "ABBA" Parent would be.

Only for very special reasons at special times, for the good of all, does God miraculously set aside the usual laws of nature, as they normally are meant to apply for all equally.

For evil attributed to God, is primarily caused from the way we treat or misuse others, such as in greed, racism, sexism, and all kinds of negative passions and selfish desires.

Especially damaging to so many by those in positions of power, as well as those around us, who have put themselves above an equal concern for others, they live and work with.

Some believe, including myself there is a separate but not human, intelligent negative spirit in our world, who is so selfish; it goes around deliberately attempting to take the will of those who it can or who will lean towards evil.

Whether there actually is or not, really matters little as to the damage we see, whether "the devil made me do it" is true; as humans have proven themselves capable of the worse with or without any outside help!

There are many, many negative things we can have happen to us and for most much will happen in each one's normal lifetime here.

As well as it is possible to experience many good things just in the living, unless we become too hurt, discouraged and close off our heart and feelings.

Such as those of us fortunate enough to be able to read, as many will not have that opportunity. Some because of birth, as well as free will choices we make ourselves, but most because of only a few, with too much selfish control in the world, who directly affect most lives right now, in many hard to know ways!

We have been advised by most of the world's good prophets, when possible, to stay away from negative harmful, or what we may believe are sinful, bad actions. Especially if there is nothing we are able to do to make them more positive, for they can or will try to diminish us, draw us away from feeling God's equal love for us.

Yet just because we are interrelated, we are our brothers, (sisters) keepers, Better we go towards the best than the worse, for it does us no good to stick our heads in the sand or think there is an Island that will always be safe, outside of Heaven.

What we have done or failed to do, in the keeping of our world family as well as our personal family, can increase or decrease our Spirits or Souls.

Unlike spirits of evil, who may try to manipulate or control you, The Spirit of The Living God will never try to take away your free will. Be suspicious of the motives of anyone who does try to take your free will away.

To make you a slave is the work of the evil that is in this world for it has no feelings for you or for your rights!

Don't assume evil does not have intelligence, whether it is in a person, or just in a spirit form, it may even try to put negative thoughts into your head, but can only hear what you say, and cannot know what you are thinking. Guess, or deduct maybe, but pretty sure only God can know your thinking at any one time. At least like to think so. Maybe I just don't really want to know the answer to that for sure, because I don't.

We each have a need for a spiritual guide within us, as well as without, to help confirm what is best for us, on our path to the fullness of Truth.

Parents or Caretakers are our first spiritual guides, by what they do, as well as what they say. In adulthood the best spiritual guides can be real friends too.

It is my belief we can be more easily misled by evil spirits, if we do not consciously connect with the Loving Spirit of God, to warn us of their deviousness or danger.

Some may think of this connection as just our better Intuition, like a sixth sense, or it may seem to be from your formed conscience, others may have given you. This may be true to some extent, as what is inner or outer can be misunderstood, but if it is not a Holy Love, you are likely to be misled.

The Living Loving Creator, the God of all, loves us as a Perfect Parent would love a child, and whom we can depend upon to help us when it may be a matter of life or death, with the strength to live the best possible life.

As long as we are willing and when we are willing, for few there are, who are willing all the time, or who can manage all the time to follow where such a Spirit of Holy Love leads. Infallibility is not a human trait.

People in our past or who now influence us, may not have known this. That is why we need to confirm for ourselves with the best, if we are not sure, or we can chance being misled, by something else that is less!

Most of us are trained by a school of thinking, or by our culture, to think and act from the part of our brain, which is called our logical or reasoning side. By reasoning from just this side of our brain, our human logic tends to tells us this world is just a slightly civilized jungle and "might is what makes what is right" or even "who owns the gold makes the rules".

There is of course, some truth to this, but there is the side of the brains way of thinking, sometimes called the more God like part, where most of us can go to, that can give us wisdom to better experience and more balance the best and truth in reality.

There can even be sensed a kind of inner and outer love that is always saying: "Love One Another", "even your enemies". For this is the way to make friends instead of enemy's", for the best kind of life and for the living of it!

The best way, what is better for all, are Equal Rights, Equal Respect, and Concern. Equal opportunity, that is the "Equality" God gave me to share, and the accepting of it is needed, to go towards a joyful inner peace.

What I have learned about such "intuition" is that most of us seem to be born with it, but most Patriarchal cultures put it down, for it comes not from just your "logical" brain, but from the intelligence of what we call "Heart".

Not a "Macho" word and sometimes even considered a sissy word. Yet every cell in every physical body can connect to that kind of intelligence and can give us wisdom from a spiritual source of being, even from God.

Another word "New Agers" or believers in this Aquarian Age might use is "Cosmic Consciousness". I like that concept too, but prefer the term The Holy Spirit, who Jesus said we were to let guide us to the fullness of Truth and he told Believers to wait till they received the "rebirth" of God's Spirit before "going out" into the world.

To connect with an Intelligent Spiritual Consciousness or one's intuition, is like having an inner compass, or a 6th sense, but not just from the logic side of the brain. It can come through any of your regular senses of seeing, hearing, tasting, smelling, or can be a feeling in your gut, as well as your heart, that something is right, or wrong to do, or just not the time to do.

To "See" with an inner eye, is also called the God Eye.

There is a known specific God Eye center right between and above the eyes, and has now been scientifically tested or electrically stimulated to allow people to more easily see into the spiritual world, but for thousands of years that part of the brain has been known as a doorway to the Spirit beyond self.

How did they know that?

You might want to ask a Holy One from India. It is found in their scriptures, from thousands of years ago! This sense can be an over all "knowing" something might be right to do, that is not logically, scientifically explained.

One of the ways to increase or develop this sense is to listen, or be in the present, rather then just staying in the active thinking part of the brain, which is often being in the past or future and not in the present.

When we just stay in our reasoning side or talking to ourselves part of our brain, we are going over and over past known information, and thinking what we did or didn't do or should or should not be doing in the future, and we are not really living in the Present, where Reality Is Being.

People who are willing to balance this logic and thinking with their listening, to what is happening here and now, can live in the present and will see more, than those who are living just in the past, or future, by their logical thinking only and not connecting with what is happening in the present.

Being aware of Holiness=Wholeness presence, is having a Godly Sense!

Many have tried to live without this balance of living in the present, such as being too much in the past, or in the future, or in unbelief, eventually life tends to get the better of you. At least that happened to me at one time.

Listening for God's Holy Spirit in your heart can connect you with more than you can possible know from just using your own logic.

How can you listen to that side of your intelligence more? You get in the habit, each day of listening and being in wonder about what ever you see around you, in the present.

Being open to seeing beyond the obvious what is also behind the scene.

Wondering about what ever comes to your mind, simple or complex things it doesn't matter, what matters is to be open to wonder, and then not try to logically figure it out, but to listen to what you hear, or see, with all your senses as well as your heart.

You should start to get answers when you are trying to be open to seeing whatever, there is to "see". Don't limit the time to let the answers come to you. Daily ask your inner guidance to lead you to knowing what you need to do to get to where, you best could be.

When you feel like you have a response, trust it and do it, or work towards doing it. After a while it becomes most natural, with little or no effort.

You need to experience this for yourself.

Don't give up but keep trying, till you do feel you are connecting or getting some answers that feel right and true.

We have by nature this inner guidance, but when we stay too much on the logical side of thinking and do not listen to what our creative intuitive side is saying, we not only tend to become ridged and close minded, but we shut out what we need to hear, from our creative source!

Instead of becoming more and more enlightened we fumble around in the dark of our limited human knowing.

But like turning a light on, we can become open to being enlightened, by being willing to listen for what you most need to know, to get to where you would most like to be.

Almost like a muscle click in the opening up of the God Center in your mind, you can seek knowledge there by remembering to go there.

This should only be consciously done with the awareness that you want to work only with A God of Holy Love, not with any kind of a lesser god.

For there are lesser spiritual beings that will try to mislead you if you allow them. They may even pretend to be an Angel of Light, but there is always something below the surface of everything, and to see the fullness of things, you need to look behind the surface, to make sure what is real.

When your heart is in a righteous place you will sense something is missing or not right. If it is from a negative spiritual source, you can also cast it out with the sign of the Cross in Jesus name, if you believe in such a Holy Godly Love.

The best way to be sure not to be fooled, is to keep your heart committed to a righteous loving life, for to seek the spirit world with less, would end up costing you much more in the long run anyway.

Part of the problem of discerning, is that it takes not only God's choice as to the best time to speak to an individual, as well as to the whole, but also each one's being willing and free to hear in the heart, which controls much of what the head can hear or comprehend!

The Bible, as well as any other kind of Scriptures considered sacred, can be misunderstood with disasters, or hell in the making, depending on where your heart as well as your head is. There is reason to believe that what is put into the Spirit world is returned up to 100 fold, in this life or the next, for evil as well as for good.

Accepting what is in God's time rather than our own can help, and avoid wrong conclusions too. As in the getting to know God you must be willing to invest your self with faith, such as a child has with a parent, even with faith unseen, such as the faith one has, who believes they are loved.

This is not to imply that the learning of God's many ways are simple, even though they may seem so, with a child like faith.

All good kinds of Scriptures from the Spiritual world, may have inspired words meant or given for that time, but comes in the ways of understanding of that time. The question we must deal with in our times, is to be able to distinguish what in Scriptures, or our cultural, religious upbringing, are actually specifically from God.

Today in our still sexist patriarchal culture, our prejudices are also still incorporated into many of our ways of speaking and thinking, such as pronouns (He, His) we use for God being commonly used male terms.

Although pronouns when used to mean God are Capitalized, and are to include the Feminine qualities of God. Found in an unabridged Webster's Dictionary.

But because God is spoken of in male terms and seen in Pastors, Priest, and as the "Godly" head of most political and secular offices, as just male, or written about only in male terms, the minds Image of God from childhood is easily pictured as just being male, leaving females to seem to be less than, or of lesser importance.

We have this inbred cultural sexism that is not so easily changed, and until we see the change as the better way, the only way to have Equal Rights and begin to end the imbalance of inequality.

We can see we are in the process of changing too, as we grow and evolve in Love and understanding.

Sexist or Patriarchal thinking of God as male only, is not only a form of Idolatry, it misinterprets God's Word as God not being equally concerned for all.

That both are created in the "Image of God" is stated in the first chapter that is the official Priestly version of Creation, and also repeated in another tribal and third,

version of Creation, in the fifth Chapter of Genesis. Both say male and female are created in the Image of God.*
*Genesis Chapter 1:27; and Chapter 5:1.

There are three known separate Creation stories combined in Genesis, and not, as many have assumed, only one seemingly continuous Creation story. The way the chapters are combined in later translations reflects it was not done accidental and written by males only.

It is the Creation story of one of the other tribes of Israel, in Chapter two* that is used to justify sexism. Starting in the 4th verse of Genesis 2:4*, some versions will have a little note such as (~), as a sign of a new version.

This more often repeated second story is from another tribe and is known theologically to be a parable about how evil came into our world in the form of a talking snake.

What kind of snakes do you know that actually talk? I've known a few, but of the human kind.

In the male dominating culture of Biblical times there needed to be stories told by males at the nightly campfires to downplay that children were created or born of females to justify their sexism and inequality.

Told hundreds of years before being written down. The female in the story is said to be the one tempted by the talking snake as well as the first one to sin, who of course was the one who convinced the man to sin, and so is given the punishment by God to be the one to bear the pain of childbirth because of her "sin". On top of it all, her wisdom is thereafter not to be trusted, for convincing the man to sin!

This added, but understood in theology as the non-official, version has served sexism well, and is still being used by many in power to justify their male control, as from the mouth of God.

Another red flag to it not being a literal or real story of creation, but a male version to explain their right to a patriarchal male ruled culture, is that it has a different order of Creation than the first and official Priestly Creation version. For in the second version it is the man who is Created first, before the animals, and then woman being created to serve him or to be used by him.

It may take not only a historical knowledge of theology but a loving or Godly heart to discern rightly. In the same way as many Scriptures can be misused or misunderstood as coming from God when they may have added male traditions and customs of inequality, or forms of sexism from those times.

In the first Creation story, the official Priestly version, it should be noted the original word translated for "day" also meant an age or era of time, and not a specific 24-hour time limit as usually translated.

Genesis has at least 3 versions of Creation written down hundreds, thousands of years, after being passed on, as stories told orally at campfires.

There is Archeological evidence of earlier cultures, before this present male Patriarchal culture began, evidences of Matriarchal cultures for thousands of years, before the last 5000 years of this Patriarchal age. Their images of God before then were mostly female and often they were pregnant females.

The much later written down book of Genesis, somewhere in the middle part of the Patriarchal age, not until 2-3,000 years ago, as a collection of Creation stories and Hebrew genealogies taken from the different 12 tribes, stories they handed down, but not finally officially written down, on parchment scrolls, until somewhere between 1000-500 B.C. by the all male Scribes and Priests.

The story of "Beginnings" or Genesis, was placed first in the Bible, but is one of the last to be written as part of the Jewish Covenant, that is before the Christian Covenant and the Gospels were written. Both written by males as the only ones allowed at that time to write.

In the Equalitarian Age, all must be given the opportunity to learn to read or write, to have a chance to become the best they can be. Partly how inequality has gained such an unfair advantage of so many people in the world, male as well as females! What human greatness we may have already missed out on!

By the time of the Christian reformation, the Monk/Priest and Scholar, Martin Luther, decided on only 66 of the Biblical Books as being inspired. Later in the Council of Trent, the Bishops of the Catholic Church voted in a total of 73, considered as the official inspired books.

These differences, of which books are considered part of the Sacred Scriptures, have helped to create the numerous sects within Christianity, with many hundreds of denominations at present.

Worldwide some Scriptures are considered sacred to some and not to others, a big cause of past, as well as current conflicts, another form of inequality, a lack of equal respect.

Jesus is reported to have said we are to "Worship in Spirit and in Truth" *. *John 4:23,24

To do that we first have to allow The Holy Spirit of God, into our own heart, mind, and soul who leads us to the fullness of Truth. Humans as a whole, many individuals can't be trusted to have it, or trust that God's Spirit is being first in their lives.

Yet we also need other believers and seekers to share and grow in truth with, to feel and to be a part of the whole, and to learn from the whole, so don't forsake fellowship, unless your called to be a desert Monk.

Best to know our history, to be able to see the inspired Scriptures as Covenants from God in a time and place, and then to trust The Living God within, as well as without, to help in guiding us to the fullness of Truth for our time.

Most people's religions have a Covenant or Creed, the members accept when joining, often at a young age, before the knowing of other beliefs.

In this way most religious cultures are passed down from one generation to the next.

As reading and writing is learned, so should there be some understanding of the different religious beliefs and what they share in common.

The original words of Christian Scriptures have been elaborated on, interpreted and translated into our more complex languages of today that required adding the translators defining or the meaning of his time, as to what the originals actually said.

Such as the word for blood brother, cousin, or step-brother being the same word in the originals, and was not usually differentiated, as we do today with our more specific word meanings, one of the reasons why we have so many different versions, and interpretations.

Most of our earliest Christian scriptures date only from 315-325 AD, from the first Roman Council of the Catholic Church, several hundreds of years after the time of Jesus. These are now kept in the Vatican Vaults in the Library under Vatican City.

Much of history, culture, we know have been written by males, primarily for males, those who were the victors of violence then in control, or were appointed or approved by the males in power at the time.

Only a few or partial pages can be dated as any of earlier originals. Yet it is the original words from God that count and why discernment from God's Holy Spirit, and confirmation from The Golden Rule are needed.

The Creator of all people, things, would seem to be the only kind of God worthy of our worship.

"ABBA" Jesus said, meaning our Heavenly Parent, would have an equal concern for all, the weakest as well as the strongest. How many will be judged worthy to enter Heaven, the way they treated even the least*. *Matthew 25:40

AH, THE ROMANTICS OF ROME

Awoke early this morning from the noise of two lovers quarreling, three floors below my street window. Was it too much of a Saturday night party?

Too much Alcohol? Sounds, looks like it! Her tears flowing as he paces up and down. As his anger increases, it ebbs, and then starts up again. He seems to be saying this is all her fault, over and over; they play that alcoholic duet, back and forth. Under the influence of their demons of intoxication violence is always near.

As the sun chases the shadows away he continues to rant and rave, off and on he checks his pockets, then searches her purse, it becomes obvious they must have lost their very last euro's!

Maybe they were robbed, spent too much, or even a pickpocket may have taken their money, anyway it is somehow all her fault! The money, the very last of their money is gone. There is no more, just somehow all gone!

Why doesn't one of them just walk away, start anew, at least until another day?

Maybe they have nowhere to walk to?

They must both be in shock to just stay here when there is nothing obviously left now of their once, only hours ago hot romantic night. Now the dislike is just as strong with seemingly no love left between either of them for right now anyway.

No respect or concern either. Yet marching back and forth, he continues to rant and rave, she mostly weeps.

Both are caught up in an unseen web of frustration consternation, accusations, anger, sad weeping, a continuous wringing of hands.

Turning to and then away from each other, than turning back again to what might have been, now away, from even a hope left for what once was theirs.

I could not watch it anymore, as even a hungry seagull began to chime in. Thank Goodness by the time I dressed, got downstairs and out the door, they were gone.

At this early time I could now escape the more than normal rush to St. Peters, that would soon began, today being a special day of Blessing for Pope John Paul II, who had once promised hope to the thousands of religious, mostly Sisters, who came to St. Peter's Square, way back in 1979, to ask for an end to their discrimination within The Church.

He had promised them, he was going to do what he could, in memory of his namesake, John Paul I. Yet many years later in 1984, he announced that Jesus had only appointed males to serve at the altar!

In spite of evidence to the contrary; but most would have been in non-public gatherings and have not been as well known, but known by any well trained Catholic Theologian. Surely a Pope would know.

Still many Mary Magdalene Churches in Southern France where she fled, or was cast out, with several others, not only from the Jewish persecution in Jerusalem but tradition says from Peter as well. In one famous Church near where she is believed to have lived in a cave for a while, they keep her skull in one of the side altars.

At the time of Jesus, women by Jewish laws, could be stoned for even talking to a male outside their family, let alone preach.

They could not go into the synagogues, or main Temple but had to remain in the outer courts with the other slaves. In very conservative Synagogues and Mosques, they are still not allowed inside, but must stay in an outer court. The men make all the "moral" decisions, even including whether to have one or more wives!

Once, when John Paul II was on Television in the news, I cried out to God to know why he was refusing to put into practice the Pastoral part of Vatican II, to "end discrimination within The Church". I suddenly saw a vision, of his hands tied behind his back, with a knife suspended in the air, about a foot away; it would stay for just a few seconds!. We are no longer under the canon laws of Vatican I but under Vatican II, but most now in control, have been indoctrinated into the false idolatry of male superiority, partly sucked in by the running together of the first two creation stories, to make them seem as one story. Even St. Paul may have been, if he actually wrote all that is attributed to him. Who can know for sure? Most Biblical words were not decided upon until the Council in Rome, under Emperor Constantine between 315-325AD.

The difference in the writing, in some of his letters does indicate later writers, writing under his name. At that time a fairly common practice for writers, who were not well known, to write under a known Apostle's name!

I had felt John Paul II natural charisma and he did help the Workers Unions in Poland, in resisting the oppression they were facing then, as a Bishop there. His support for the workers Unions, at that time gives me mixed emotions about him.

By arriving at St. Peter's this early I had a chance to share a mass with just a few of some of the faithful, at one of the side Altars. We knelt on the cold marble floor to be near the altar, as the host is offered in Thanksgiving.

In the sharing of Christ peace you can see in their faces the feast had refreshed and fed us for another busy day, except not so much for me this time, as I must still have those two who were below my window, rambling, stuck in my mind.

Walking out of St. Peters Basilica looking over the huge Piazza of St. Peters Square, I could see the crowds coming in from all directions.

Going down the left stairs to the side between the tall now decorated giant circular columns, tried to say the first decade of the Joyful Mysteries of the Rosary.

As the crowds increased the noise level seemed to become almost a roar in my head, till I could not hear my own inner voice, in trying to contemplate Jesus presentation as a child in the temple.

Knowing a quieter place to be able to meditate on these mysteries, I slipped out to the outer side of the Vatican walls, away from the crowds and began the walk all around the outside of the high walled Vatican City.

A long walk, of going way up the hill, around, and then back down, one of those many "7" hills of Rome, taking me at least an hour or more. Several times I had felt the need to do this. Amazing how small the state of Vatican City actually is!

After attempting but mostly failing to contemplate, and only finishing the joyful and one or two of the sorrowful mysteries, I tried to come back into St. Peter's Square but could not, the crowds seemed so dense, and it felt more like entering onto a carnival grounds than a sacred place. Just did not want to be a part of this at all.

So by noon found myself back in my room wondering why I had not stayed? At least I could have stayed as a Witness, and now feeling very selfish.

Maybe if I had had more courage today, more belief, that it was not as hopeless, as it just all seemed right then?

Repentance and acceptance came only after being led to read, "Holiness consist simply in doing God's will, and being just what God wants us to be." St. Therese.

HALF WAY THROUGH

Last Day of April, only half way through the Prayer and Fasting for this time in Rome. Just couldn't put on sackcloth or fast today, with very little prayer.

Fighting off a cold, it has been raining again most of the day. Had thought earlier about trying to go to the Vatican, and even ventured out between rains this morning to see how strong I felt about walking but ended up spending most of the day in bed with just a little work on the computer.

Trying to rewrite a now realized not so good poem I did many years ago, called "Idolatry" of which there seems to be so much going on here,

With the Image of The late Pope John Paul II much bigger than life, between every one of the numerous columns that line St. Peter's Square, as well as in many Church's throughout the City of Rome.

Huge outdoor movie screens flash his Image and play continuously his many trips worldwide, they show him being adored by crowds of thousands wherever he went.

Now thinking about what God had shown me, if he felt his hands were tied maybe that is why he chose to hang on for the last possible moment before leaving, thinking he might be able to outlive the one or ones, holding the knife at his back?

I think I will choose that probability for his actions, knowing towards the end of his life, at least the last 12 years, he must have suffered a lot.

At last weeks Wednesday audience in St. Peter's Square, Our now Pope Benedict XVI did seem to notice my sackcloth outfit when his Pope Mobile slowly passed by.

But this time his guards refused to take my paper, it was the same one I had mailed to him at the Vatican Post Office two days before, so they probably do have it. In essence it just said this:

For Holy Father Pope Benedict XVI,

"At this time in history, if our moral inequality isn't obvious to you, the state of the world economics should be.

All of the systems are obviously on very shaky ground; at least a spiraling downfall by just their printing paper money with nothing to back it with but unrepayable debt.

Can you understand and feel the need to put our prayers and intentions towards ending all the inequality responsible for this situation?

Inequality is the unfair belief that perpetuates the greed and elitism that is killing us spiritually, and physically.

Today at least one-third and more, of all people are being forced to live on a slow starvation diet. Thousands of God's Children will actually starve to death today, with millions more going to bed hungry.

It was when all had seemed lost, many years ago in the Church, after the death of Pope John Paul I, the Holy Spirit spoke to me the one word of "Equality".

Now, for years I have felt the need to go to the root of the problem to treat others with equal fairness, God's "Equality".

One of our world's moral makers being the Catholic Church, as the primary holder of the largest number of Christian's world wide, continues against their own Canon law from Vatican II, Pastoral Constitution, article 29 + others that say there shall be no more discrimination for either sex or race...as not the Will of God.

Yet the practice of inequality for the female half of God's people, is being continued, in essence saying the female Image of God is not in Christ, so cannot be ordained within this male only run Church!

Sincerely,

Betty C. Dudney

HUNGER

I am so Hungry, having a hard time with this fasting of two meals a day, and won't get my saved noon meal until after 5 pm. A Couple hours from now! Feels like starving.

So talked myself into drinking a cup of Ginger tea right now. Also had an orange from dinner of couple days ago, earlier this afternoon.

It is so much easier to fast when I am in a Church or at the fountain, in St. Peter's Square praying. To be always hungry is such a drag, I only feel that kind of hunger when fasting a lot.

My oldest daughter tells me about feeling it frequently as she is often trying to curb her appetite by fasting to keep her weight down.

Eventually it seems to wear you down, and you have an almost uncontrollable need to feast. Yet I am trying to stay in solidarity with those who are literally starving, with no choice.

To pray for them, asking God to give them comfort and the strength to go on till we can end this terrible needless inequality of those who are now on a starvation diet of one or less meals per day.

Turned to Psalm 130:6:
"My soul waits for The Lord"

GOD AS THE BREATH OF LIFE
Boundless and without end, God can be known as Infinite, Freeing
LOVE, PEACE, and JOY.
HOLY LOVE, EQUITY, A GOD who is
"Not a god of partiality".
Nor is the cause of evil.

Some human causes are the act of putting one's Self
Above an equal concern for others.
God as One, infinite, yet can Live in each heart.

I am trying to break free from my own cultural conditioned kind of thinking, to be able to express more of God's way of "Equality" thinking, knowing words can be so easily misunderstood. Partly by where our hearts or motives are, but also from where our morality comes from.

Slavery, Sexism, all kinds of inequality, have been the patriarchal morality. All the way up to the very top of our pyramids of control, there is such a lack of equality, enforced by the cultural mostly patriarchal laws!

One of the reasons humility is so important when seeking Holiness is because it comes from a word that means Our Wholeness. As a way of seeing, understanding, even sympathizing with how we all sin or fall short daily, by what we do or fail to do and yet each are still equally loved by a God of unconditional love!

If we sin by being self-righteous, how can we think we are much better than others? Or for that matter much worse, than any other? Especially if we had to "walk in their shoes" as the saying goes?

Humility is partly recognizing the Equality we do share with each other as being created in God's Image!

It is Pride, a big source of inequality said to be the first sin of evil that wants to put our individual selves on a pedestal or to put others below us in inferior positions, to assert our will to have our own way. It could just be to make us feel better about ourselves, even at the expense of others. Pride will rear its head when we are only considering self.

We can experience the opposite when we ourselves have been put down too often as not being thought of as enough and then we can have a lack of self worth or very little self-confidence that tends to make us think others are so much better! We will then tend to put others on a pedestal and negate ourselves, even to the point of harm.

Another form of pride is thinking we deserve more than others because we feel we have been favored or have more in some way such as talents, good looks, or money, and have yet to know as Jesus warned: those given much, much more will be expected from them.

Best to see our reality from an unselfish way, not how we might sometimes feel like lording it over others or to shy away from doing what we can, when or where needed.

Selfishness and greed can make it seem justified to take more than what we need or not want to share fairly with others but will leave us later to face the misery of selfish decisions and actions, that have done harm to others.

Very hard to break habits of this kind of thinking we may have learned from the way we have been treated by those who may or may not have been able to love, or seemed at the time to care much about us.

Yet as we keep evolving, growing in knowledge and spiritual maturity, we can't help but become aware of our own "Equality". It is a God given right of Freedom that is written into most people's normal nature to want, even cherish those Equal Human Rights that stop only at the Equal Rights of others

LAST TIME IN ROME

Another general Pope Audience while witnessing here in Rome. Hearing a lot of good words but no specific action noted and this is last time it will be possible to be here, at least for now.

Did manage again to get close enough to the railings when the Pope passed, to get another letter to one of the guards who walk around and behind the Pope Mobile, he is up too high to be able to give it to him personally.

Again the Pope came by the section near where I was last week, this time he circled two times around, and he did make eye contact at least once; it was just not a very pleasant look, which I would have preferred.

Oh well, if I were him I probably wouldn't like me either.

Yet ours is not a personality contest but means the life and death of so many. This decision he must make, of practicing inequality or "Equality" for the female half of God's Image.

I am feeling worn out and still sick, with this devilish Shingles and need to go home. Till we both meet on our Day of Judgment I will pray for you our Pope, to be free from the Antichrist.

Thank Goodness, Praise God, I am actually here on this plane. May I never have to come again, at least not to witness here. Have learned to love Rome in all its specialness, as well as the little of the countryside that I have been able to see, which has a completely different feel, even the long stretch of road from the Airport into the city.

Twice I did go for the day to the hot Springs, way out into the heart of the beautiful country that looks a lot like some of Tennessee and parts of the South. Even to ride on a daily free bus from the nice resort that owns the hot springs near the ancient volcano.

In another direction, another time, rode up into other Roman hills to see the heard about uncorrupted body of St. Clare, who was St. Francis lifelong friend, and great spiritual worker too.

Hard to tell how uncorrupted her body actually is, being able to see it only from a distance most likely for her protection, as it is laying open on an altar, but looks from where it is roped off like it is.

Makes me thankful for having been able to be so close to St. Giuseppe, to be able to sit beside his glass coffin, at one of the side altars where I could sit on a step and be right beside him.

Realize it is still possible it could just be a waxed representation but doesn't matter anymore with the miracle I experienced that day he was made a Saint, for now know in Spirit form he does lives on.

ECONOMIC EXPLORATION

The poverty and misery of so many people in our world today does not point just to their personal efforts but primarily to our unequal distribution systems, the misuse, unfair use, of most of the world's resources for so long now.

Some want to not claim any of the blame or responsibility for the actions of others, especially those of long gone ancestors.

Yet everyone wants to receive as much from his or her ancestors as has been passed on in general, socially or legally and most of us do not want to see this as a moral contradiction.

We all have a physical nature that tends to be selfish or self centered, a big part of our lesser natures, just as being spiritual is part of our higher nature, our Holy = Whole nature.

It is our spiritual nature to want to be equally or fairly treated, as well as to treat others with equal fairness and this nature is found even in children. This is a natural, universal moral law, most people, in most religions or beliefs, call the Golden Rule!

When we are willing to follow this Golden Rule of caring about our selves as we care for others, we begin to develop an Equal, whole, or Holy Love for all.

This Spirit of Holy Love, helps us to see ourselves as equally part of the whole, and makes it easier to be in harmony, with not only our own being, but to feel a harmony with others too!

Each person, as a human being has the basic right to food, for shelter, and the chance to become the best each has a talent to be able to be.

In exchange this comes with a responsibility, for each to help contribute to the whole where possible, first by the normal desire to develop each ones own talent or ability.

Just being human is a justifiable reason for such a safety net, just as taxes can be justified when used for collective needs such as fire and police protection, or for the physical security of the community as a whole.

We need to have Judges to be able to settle our personal disputes, with enforcement people to mediate laws as to what can or cannot be allowed to infringe on others equal rights, to be able to live together and share the benefits, as well as the dangers.

To prevent any more dictatorial or bought elections, we need councils for local, state, national, or international groups chosen as being knowledgeable in some qualifying field, possibly by lot, when more apply then are needed, much as voters are now called for jury duty, with expenses and at least a minimum decent salary, plus the use of specialized staff advisors for help.

A true Citizen's government, with minimum of 2 and maximum 4-8 year terms possible, depending on interest, with the safeguards of a voters recall.

Another possibility for voters are equally paid commercials for people running, who get enough petitions signed?

Must also be other ways to keep money from buying elections?

CHRISTIAN TEACHINGS ON LABOR, AND UNIONS

Excerpts from Catholic Social Teaching on Labor, Unions, and Workers Rights:

"In the first place, the worker must be paid a wage sufficient to support him and his family."

Quadragesimo Anno (The Fortieth Year) #71 On Reconstruction of the Social Order, Pius XI, 1931:

"We consider it our duty to reaffirm that the remuneration of work is not something that can be left to the laws of the market place; nor should it be a decision left to the will of the more powerful". Pope John XXIII, 1961:

"It must be determined in accordance with justice and equity; which means that workers must be paid a wage which allows them to live a truly human life and to fulfill their family obligations in a worthy manner."

Mater et Magistra (Te Mother and Teacher) #71 Economic Justice for All #303: Pastoral Letter on Catholic Social Teaching and the U.S. Economy, U. S. Catholic Bishops, 1986:

"The Church fully supports the right of workers to form unions or other associations to secure their rights to fair wages and working conditions. This is a specific application of the more general right to associate."

"Work is in the first place for the worker and not the worker for work. Work itself can have greater or lesser objective value, but all work should be judged by the measure of dignity given to the person who carries it out."

Laborem Exercens (On Human Work) #6 John Paul II, 1981:

"It is right to struggle against an unjust economic system that does not uphold the priority of the human being over capital and land".

Centesimus Annus (The Hundredth Year) #35 John Paul II, 1986

"REPETITION AND CHANGE"

"Repetition and Change", that is all there is, some say! "Repetition, Repetition, Repetition, and then a little Change"! A Catholic Priest from India shared this with me.

Repetition repeated so many times it becomes easy, feels natural, it is the way we learn most things. Change does not come so easy. Creating a positive society change can be hard to do without putting legal as well as moral safeguards in place.

For those who enjoy control over others, it will seem for them easier to mistreat or to take advantage, then to treat others with equal fairness, even to think of them as having equal rights, unless there are legal safeguards that can be appealed to, especially when there is long standing customs of race, sexual, or social inequality.

Each generation has the responsibility of having to deal with any threat to their Freedoms or Equal Rights. They must watch for misuses that twist their rights into a "double speak", or they chance losing them.

This can also happen when we choose to look the other way or stop being willing to help others, those who we see or know are in need, such as in people mistreating others, bullies, or because of prejudices, discriminations, and economic inequalities, where strong social, as well as legal protections are needed.

Aloha is a word used in the Hawaii Islands to say a simple Hello or Goodbye, but it means to their culture, so much more than just that. Aloha is about the showing of high regard of each other.

By the respecting of each one's differences and still being able to recognize the many commonalities we share, each in our diversities.

There is no reason to put others down for their sexual differences for we would in reality be putting part of our own nature down. For all humans, we know from scientific evidence, inside each do have both female as well as male qualities, male and female hormones, with one or the other in predominance.

Once I learned most animals have about the same amount of natural sexual preference for the same sex, as humans do anywhere from 7-11% I had to give up my own homophobia as it seemed logical that is the way God created us, or is a part of our natural variances!

Some want to deny it by saying in animals it is just a way of showing dominance, but call it rape or consensual, it is still a sexual act.

Others rationalize it to be a misuse of their beliefs. That may partly be because of today's meanings that we attach to the different original Biblical meanings in those days.

They had more, other and different meanings in their language, and different customs of Biblical times, such as in the parable story of Sodom and Gomorrah, being about a Godly visit to Lot to leave a wicked town.

In those days the understanding of desert tribal hospitality demanded that no harm come to strangers, as they were treated as sacred or usually considered to be like God, or from God, with a special message for those they chose to visit.

As few humans would have been able to survive travel in that desert wilderness unless in a caravan, or group being about the only way to travel in those days.

In the story they promised to lead Lot out of the city, before it was going to be destroyed. So to turn them over to a drunken crowd it seemed better for Lot to sacrifice his own daughters, and he did offer them up to the crowd, rather than his two "guest from Heaven".

In their escape, Lot's wife was turned into a pillar of Salt for looking back! This all taking place near the Dead Sea, one can see there, many clumps of evaporated salt along the edges, some did look, in my twice passing that area, a little like pillars or statues but more likely were caused from the winds and evaporating Dead Sea.

This is a parable of a still current custom of desert Arabs to treat travelers with a Royal or Godly welcome, at least for the first few days of a visit!

Should the majority anywhere feel threatened by allowing equal rights to others, to a lesser minority?

The possibility of sexual harm does exist, but in all forms of sexual behavior, promiscuity for health reasons, just as when there is a taking advantage of age, size, where there is no consent, are forms of inequality we call rape, of either sex.

MESSAGE TO OUR NEW POPE FRANCIS

Trying to look behind the surface, after the original joy of being given another Holy Francis to serve The Church.

Lately seeing a little into the depth of his aloneness in his believing how few are going to be willing to join him with the change it will take to get His Bishops, let alone the Cardinals into the Equalitarian Age. I believe he will try. I also know God's Hand will be there helping where most needed. We need to do our part those who are aware to help where possible.

Sent this letter the 12 of May of 2013, not long after the new Pope's reign began.

Your Holiness Pope Francis,

Others, sometimes acting in The Pope's place, have been part of the problems within The Church and may continue as where the antichrist seems to prefer best, to try to foil God's plans. Sometimes in miraculous ways, God has insisted that I keep trying for the last 40 years, to convince The Church of it's need, and for our world to turn away from inequality, to end our cause of discrimination.

The Holy Spirit also so inspired the Bishops in our last World Council especially in The Pastoral Constitution of Vatican II, as there are many passages that point to our need to: "end the discrimination within The Church as to race, sex...as not the Will of God". *Article 29 + others, Pastoral Constitution, Vatican II.

Jesus could only have come as a male, at that time 2000 years ago.

Theologians tell us God is neither just male nor just female but is A Spirit. A Spirit of Holy Love, living in both.

We biologically share, complement, and balance each other's natures, as both are created in God's Image according to the first as well as the third Creation stories of Genesis 1:27; 5:1.

In the last several years I also witnessed with another, at the fountain below Papal office windows, for three months at a time, as this was the most I was allowed to stay in Italy, fasting daily two meals in sack-cloth and praying the Rosary for an end to inequality within The Church, where God's morality should be flowing.

I believe you are close to God's Holy Spirit and will help to lead our world out of the inequality and evils of discrimination and not continue in them as the Church has for so long, at such a cost to both females as well as males.

Please keep yourself safe especially in regards to your food. Perhaps a trustworthy owner or cook from a favorite Roman Restaurant.

Stay In God's Peace, and the Joy of our promised Eternal life.

Second message, as there was no response from the first, with a requested signature this time for who ever it is delivered to.

All kind of scary, not only because it might not have been seen by the Holy Father and if this one isn't either, than I might have to go there again to personally deliver the message knowing the other Witness with the same message from God, is no longer there and unknown where she is for almost a year now.

July 1, 2013

Our Holy Father Francis,

Am Writing forty years after being given the Prophetic Word of "EQUALITY" by God's Holy Spirit.

Have witnessing to, as well as at The Vatican since 1985.

Three times to three Popes, for the ending of our inequality, discrimination, especially for the female half of God's Image. Without ending inequality within the largest of our Christian institutions how can we expect it to be ended elsewhere in our world?

Till then up to half of our world must live on daily wages of about U.S.$3.00.

Today thousands of children will continue to starve to death; millions more will go to bed hungry tonight!

Not to mention so many children will be unable to go to school to learn even to read or write because they must go to work, as young as 5-6 years old.

With up to 90% of our world's economy and resources now in the hands and control of less than 2%. Resources and Labor, God means to be used for the benefit of all.

DID GET A RESPONSE THIS TIME THAT IT HAD BEEN DELIVERED TO SOMEONE, AT LEAST, IN ROME?

Last letter to Rome in March 2014

Dear Pope Francis,

This is to request you to end the discrimination for the female half of God's Image. The message of "Equality" was given to me at my Spiritual "Rebirth" over 40 years ago.

Have witnessed to the last two former Pope's, who took the place of John Paul I, after he promised many religious women, to end inequality within The Church.

When you were elected you seemed Holy enough to do the right thing, so tried to retire but after the Mother-In-Law jokes realized you too, are caught up in the sexism of Patriarchy, the evil of male idolatry in our world, for have you ever heard of a Father-In-Law joke?

Yet, you are the one, God says who has the religious power to turn our world's morality towards a more equal and righteous one for all. Please confirm for yourself God's Will of "Equality" or inequality?

Or must I leave again, my home here in beautiful Tennessee to stand at your fountain fasting, praying for an end to discrimination, from where God's morality flows? Best possible 80th Birthday present this June, so God may finally allow me to retire in Peace.

God's Peace in Christ,

Betty C. Dudney

TRADITIONS VS. THE HOLY SPIRIT WITHIN

God's Ways are higher than man's ways". Praise God!

Many of men's ways, or traditions have been evolving for the better since primitive times such as slavery, racism, and sexism and other forms of inequality.

While those less evolved or those who have gotten so caught up in forms of addictive greed and power tripping have continued to misuse many people.

Few of us would choose to have traditions that belittle others. Most of us want to have good relationships, and are evolved enough to not want to see other human beings enslaved.

We can see, in some forms of inequality or discrimination within The Church, there has been progress such as towards ending racial discrimination.

Before Vatican II, by tradition, only Italians were elected Pope within the Roman Catholic Church. Then since Vatican II when it was officially considered to be a form of discrimination, we have had Pope John Paul II who came from Poland, Pope Benedict XVI from

Germany, and our present Pope Francis, from South America.

Racial discrimination in regards to Popes within The Church has been broken! Racism in other ways within The Church does not seem so much of a problem either, hopefully now it will not be long before sexism is no longer practiced.

A recent worldwide survey within The Church requested by Pope Francis to all Bishops, is encouraging, as probably the only such general laity participation since the first couple hundred years of Christianity. This survey could help end other forms of discrimination.

The tallied results in my own parish found only 10% did not believe women should be given identical roles and responsibilities as men, in regards to the activities and administration of the Church; only about the same small percent were against women being able to be a Priest!

It was also very encouraging to see that in social justice issues, only 6% were against the question of whether the Church has a responsibility to teach people to protect each other from poverty and from physical harm or mental abuse.

Only 8% said no to the question of "Do you think the Catholic Church has a responsibility to spend its resources helping people be able to live safely and to have adequate nutrition and healthcare?"

In other issues of cohabitation, abortion, divorce, homosexuality there was more of a split except for birth control. Only 10% were against it, or thought it a sin, and only 13% considering remarriage a sin and that being without an annulment from the Church of a valid marriage to begin with. Perhaps because it can be expensive, takes so long and requires like another court hearing, most people would find it hard to have to go through the trauma again, let alone for other reasons.

Now the question is, will there be many of the laity who will even be allowed to take this survey?

Or will the Bishops only give it to their Priest and Deacons for them to answer for their parish, excluding the laity as evidently already has happened in some areas?

Can it then be a very honest survey since each Priest future is tied to vows of doing his Bishop's Will while in his Diocese, and can find themselves back in the boondocks if in much disagreement with their Bishops politics, or way of thinking.

I can't help but hope there are enough Bishops who will allow the laity to take the survey and evidently so does this present Pope, at least his purpose to learn what present day Catholics really are hearing from The Holy Spirit as well as from the all male hierarchy. Yet some of my Catholic friends, in other parts of the country tell me they have not even heard of the survey!

Our Pope seems to want this 2014 October Synod to be a step into the 21st Century from Vatican II and he intends to address these questions he says this October and in the following October the Synods 50th anniversary in 2015.

So once again I am feeling there is nothing more to do right now but to wait and see.

It is such a right step forward for The Church to have such a survey, as long as the laity is included.

We must wait now for the repetition to end and The Holy Spirit to help us make the change, to renew The Church.

It is not just for the ending of discrimination for the female half, but an end to our sexist language, that must also occur especially within the Catholic Church as the largest and most world wide influential leader of morality and use of a patriarchal sexist language, in describing or defining God in only male pronoun terms.

For me it should be a time for much more praying but harder now to fast, yet at least once a day I am trying to do without something would otherwise reach for.

Hopefully many of you too will daily offer a prayer and think of something that wouldn't be too much to offer up too, those of you who can see our great need to end discrimination, and recognize the greater power fasting will give to your prayers. One of the most helpful, even easy ways is to pick a bad habit to give up day by day, from food to thought. Just keep trying, being the key!

There is this need to fast, at least once a day from something, for just the power to be able to stand against the negative forces that will come against all, but especially for those who may be spiritual weak or just lukewarm.

It is another one of Jesus' teachings that some things are harder to change for the better without the intensiveness of adding fasting or some sacrifice to your prayer.

Am also recognizing the results of our survey was just a small sample from one of the more progressive Parishes in the Southland of America, and may or may not be representative of others.

For a question has been, are there enough within the Church who have not been misled by the long-standing and current practice of inequality in our patriarchal culture for so many years?

I want to believe that there are enough, who choose to be led by God's Spirit, and evidently so does our present Pope, at least I believe he is honestly wanting to know what most Catholics are believing in.

For now the results of our one parish survey feel so good, a big ray of sunshine for me, in spite of the inequality for so many generations, hopefully many more have been listening to God's Holy Spirit and many are willing, to turn away from the negative harmful traditions of inequality, discriminations.

Have decided not to add the story behind S.N.A.P. here, that organization for the many sexually abused Seminarians. I have been praying for years for their peace of mind, because it was so painful to even read or hear about.

Yet is it any more painful than knowing children and adults are starving to death because of the present economic greed by so few?

Thinking that it is all somehow related together.

There is no way to know where all the blame lies on some of these universal sexual problems, in families as well as organizations, where ever anyone weaker in some way, finds themselves at the mercy of one or more uncaring, or little caring, aggressors.

Without the righteousness of the Golden Rule within most people's hearts, the consciousness of Equal Rights, Equal Concern, we would all become victims in this life, in many more ways than now.

A measure of each one's responsibility and maturity starts with becoming aware, first to our own degree of selfishness when we leave little time, energy, or resources, to do what we can to help others less able.

"An ounce of prevention is worth a pound of cure", my partly American Indian, Grandmother sometimes said to us.

She being mostly English, while my other Grandmother was mostly Irish, but having some Scottish ancestors too.

Former slaves from the South, also took some of our ancestral American last names.

It has made it easier for me to identify with many races.

If we look back in our ancestry for even a few hundred years, we can see many of us are the end result of several races or more.

Turning racial pride around has become my own source of pride, to consider myself as being a typical American Mongrel, from people who came to this land to seek a better life, and people are still coming here with that hope. For those of us here it is our turn to help now.

Racism, like Nationalism gives a sense of identity that too often turns into being a way to exclude others, with any cultural kinds of differences.

Usually out of fear or uncertainty of whether another's ways will be a hindrance or even a threat of some kind.

Not a good way to be thinking, when living in an already global economy that does best when people are free to live and work where they most want to be, or able to find their best opportunity.

Realizing it is going to be where our heart and concerns are, to how much we are going to be able to balance or equalize our own lives.

Most of us cannot go back to the one time nationalistic or tribal isolation. To avoid worldwide disasters such as nuclear wars, we must learn to turn our enemies into friends, at least tolerate or we risk widespread destruction that can take us back to being cavemen, in a desert like devastated land.

FOR PRESENT DANGERS

No more Hiroshima's, no more Japan's nuclear leaking plants and no more Chernobyl's.

Before it takes 20 years for the statistics to leak out to show how many millions of lives will be shorten because of cancer or? from these huge leaks of nuclear radiation. Unseen radiation that's all around us, lets get it back into the ground deep down, where it belongs.

No more destructible nuclear reactors, killing our oceans, polluting our agricultural land and the water supply. In fact why allow thousands of nuclear bombs that threaten all life? We now have the needed technology to detect them from satellites!

In the meantime, I have sought for the safest remedy for radiation, to take a small amount of kelp, or seaweed each day, seems best not harvested near Japan! It can be gotten in health food stores, grocery and dollar stores, sold plain or seasoned.

This helps absorb the extra radiation we all are being exposed to, some more than others. Depending upon where and how much was swept up into the upper atmosphere and where it fell, still active long after falling.

While much of the radiation settled in the areas of and around Japan, it may have already polluted as much as a third of the Pacific Ocean. A large amount has been swept up into the atmosphere where it circled the earth within days, later falling in rain, polluting water supplies, farmlands throughout the world!

There is a much stronger medicine for radiation burns but it must be individual prescribed because of the severe side effects from even a small dose of Potassium Iodine, so only for those very badly exposed.

For radiation burns, if no medical care is available, can use a teaspoon of iodized salt in a liter, or quart of water, to be sipped on during the day, this is suppose to help somewhat depending on the amount of exposure!

For the average unknown amount, a 4X4 thin wafer of seaweed should be taken daily. Seaweed, of most kinds, is a commonly eaten sea vegetable where people live near the ocean, sometimes used in salads or as a pickled garnish or relish.

It is easy to buy a seasoned seaweed wafer at a Dollar store or health food stores. My favorite is a Coconut flavored for $1.29 for 12 slices, need one a day, found on an online store at www.abe'smarket.com.

If you know you have been exposed to radiation outside shake out the outer clothing before entering inside, and best to wash them separately, then wear a different set of clothes inside.

During known fallout, stay inside as much as possible, especially for young children and youth, to minimize later birth defects. When outside better to use an umbrella, or wear wide brimmed hats, especially during known large amounts of fallout.

It is on the coastlines of the Pacific Ocean, that are most in danger of contamination being washed up at present.

Radiation coming out from the nuclear plants in Japan are still leaking into the Ocean, these leaks are expected to continue for up to 40 years, the now estimated time stated by the Company who originally built them, and who are still in charge of repairing them?

With the known potential health damage world-wide why is just this one company fixing it and not many needed resources being used to stop these leaks we know to be polluting our Pacific Ocean?

Tweets I've written, meant to send, but didn't:

Lets us pray for no more nuclear reactors or military spending for research to kill or destroy. Let us rise up as free people to live our beliefs.

Before more Hiroshima's, or nuclear fallouts insist 12,000-year radiation destruction be put back into the ground!

Or, Many of us need to pray and fast to end the inequality of more evil wars.

These tweets come to my mind, but they seem to exhaust me to think much about them, or is it tweeting can seem like, "too little too late"? Yet doesn't every little bit count? I think so.

INEQUALITY BREEDS WAR

Inequality breeds war, destruction, mistrust, Injustices of all kinds. To be able to prevent, we need moral as well as legal Equal Rights, Equal Respect, a real Concern for the needs of All.

No Cure for Peace except to "Love One Another", "even your enemies". The practice of the Golden Rule most everyone can confirm is true, deep down in the intellect of the heart.

Inequality as a belief system justifies discrimination and the taking advantage of others, allowing profits, gold, positions of power, to become like Gods.

Some of the strongest in positions of power, manage to survive at the top of the worlds present money economy, because their income is based on profits. While the majority of the people work instead for the lowest allowed minimum wages, in many places without even those minimum wages!

The workers being the ones least able to avoid the taxes, and the higher interest rates on credit cards that create a perpetual door of debt, even for the middle class, as well as for the poor.

Where even one major health issue or economic downturn can spell disaster, in a recurring cycle of stock shocks, for workers who were trying to build a retirement fund, or for the majority of investors, not in the knowing inner circle.

The few 0.1 of 1% at the top of the economic and power ladder have many well-paid staffs of Managers, Lawyers, as well as political ties that keep them in control, even from most people knowing who they are, or what they are doing.

By having the major controlling interest in many International Corporations they can chose CEO's to do Their Will over the vast number of workers, setting the standards of the amount of work and pay, throughout the world, and for this they are paid a great deal extra, in terms of not only money but also stocks and bonuses given to them, that are not available to the great majority of workers.

This is like unto a pyramid scheme, the cause of much economic and political unfairness.

A scam based on pitting and competing most people as well as nations, against each other, rather than cooperatively sharing more equitably the workers produced profits, that could and would bring much more worldwide prosperity including a stable Peace, when workers are paid a good and fair living wage.

Instead, some of the excessive profits, those actually created by the workers and buyers, are then used against them to prevent good wages, as well as many needed regulations and worker benefits.

Should our economic world be run by, or be in the control of so few? It seems for the benefit of all, many people should have the right to share more equally the profits of their own time, energy, and labor.

Our economy with a stable peace, would be something many people working together would have the power to change for the better.

"EQUALITY" is God's Answer, for Equal Respect, Equal Rights and Equal Concern. The fullness of the Universal Golden Rule, to treat others fairly, as you would most want to be treated.

It does not mean everyone should have equal amounts of anything, except for a basic universal safety net, to know physical life matters, as well as each one's Spiritual life.

Are not people more important than profits? Do we not need to have honest fair wages paid? Some will say this is not from God, but Biblical definitions tell us God is "not a god of partiality", but a God of "Equity, Mercy, Justice, Loving".

Why worship anything less?

A definition from John, one of the closest disciples of Jesus says: "God is LOVE, and when we Love, we live in God and God lives in us". I John 4:16

A HOMILY FROM A BLACK PRIEST

Heard an excellent homily this morning from a black Priest, who had been in Uganda at the time of 9/11, ten years ago.

He was speaking on today's Gospel message of Jesus teaching on forgiveness! Peter offers to forgive 7x7, thinking from his Jewish culture of an "eye for an eye", that would be a lot of forgiving. Where many of us seem to still be in! But Jesus said no matter how good and forgiving we think we are, we need to forgive at least ten times more!

This Priest mentioned, how shocked he and his people were, that such a thing as 9/11 could even happen, the destruction of so many lives, from such an act of violence.

Now ten years later, what a difference it would have made, if we had acted as a Christian nation by following the teachings of Jesus and giving our enemies and the world a great moral lesson, instead of acting in so much violence.

By doing the wiser and better thing of forgiving!

How many more lives would NOT have been lost in the wars since then? But we didn't and these wars still continue, from our "getting even" that have only made us more like the dreaded Empire of Rome in Jesus time.

We now have to live in more fear, because of all this violent destruction, and from reacting negatively to the revenge taken against our own East/West political policies, which terrorist claim caused their revengeful actions, such as in 9/11.

Could it have been caused by the U.S. government giving military aid, planes, and funds to support Israel for all these years, helping them to force, even rob the Palestinian people's land from them?

What had been their homeland for centuries, mostly Muslims but also Arab Christians, evicting them, bulldozing their homes, and pushing them into the already overcrowded West bank and desert camps, into a desolate oppression and desperation surely must have helped to create not only 9/11, but a long time Hell for hundreds of thousands of Arabs.

Are we responsible? Or those we have allowed to be over us? Those who keep most of us so much in the dark, we end up blaming the victims, the families, who have lost their homes, and the children who grow up fighting with whatever they can find to throw.

Those most responsible for the violence on both sides, keep behind the scenes, they can stay in a variety of world wide Penthouses and are known to have their own Swiss alps mountain city, with a gold reserve inside, closed to outsiders. Always safely surrounded by well paid loyal guards, with the closest workers often being family members or close in-laws.

Most citizens were and are under Big Business's media control and even some of the political sources, at that time/now, are rarely given enough information to understand all the causes or have few resources of their own to seek reconciliation for such hatred.

Seems like the average citizen has been outsmarted again, by the spirit of evil in the world, who may have even helped steal that next election from the then Senator Al Gore, a known Southern belt Christian, who did believe in forgiveness, and most likely would not have reacted in revenge, or for big oil profits for a few. What a safer place this world would be, even for Americans now.

In the past we have been so admired and looked up to, in most parts of the world, but now we can be in danger where ever we go, even in our own country, because of continuing such conflicts. Also because of this widespread retaliation and fear, we have lost most of our once cherished privacy freedoms, by the passage of laws like the Patriot Act, taking away freedoms that once made our country envied by most people in other nations.

Now we have to print money that causes what money there is, to decrease in value partly because of spending over half of our National budgets on the destructiveness of wars, the biggest financial drain for the largest military/industrial complex the world has ever seen.

Even after President Eisenhower, a former General warned us strongly against this danger as he left the office as the U.S. President just a few years ago.

How can we now somehow find the will to evolve into a more transparent government of the people, for the people? To see the need of the kind of morality that would allow us to enter Heaven here, as well as there. As the Angels say: "Peace on Earth, Goodwill to all".

UNFAIR NATIONALISM

Expanding Power and Nationalism needs war. Countries who protect all People's Equal Rights do not!

Unfair Nationalism survives by looting other country's resources. A good Freedom Loving country survives best by producing, as well as by protecting the equal rights of all.

If people want to oppose war and looting, they must oppose unfair Nationalism from those who are most promoting it, primarily the corporate war machine making industries, and the major media propaganda outlets, such as the Movies, TV and News, and others who profit from them.

At least stop the constant repeated violent commercials in prime time from being indoctrinated into the minds of our children, imprinting the idea violence is no big thing.

Dictators, and some of the International Corporations are the ones who most profit from Nationalism. Corporations by their making contracts for war machines used to kill people, often by having contracts for these war machines on both sides of the National conflicts.

So long as people hold on to practicing inequality, with the tribal notion that the young are the sacrificial fodder for war. That a few, usually males, have the right to rule others by force, instead of by the law of mutual consent, then there will be no peace among nations, or among the people!

Men with jobs can earn their needs, and then they have little incentive to loot. They will rarely have anything to gain from a war and a great deal to lose. Most people's economic interests are on the side of peace.

"It cannot be stated enough, War is only in the interest of those making the war machines with the looting of other people's natural resources".

So much is lost by this kind of destruction.

Too many people have been made the victims of the few. Universal justice or karma surely comes around from such greed and misuse of power, when enough know.

People's awareness and their being willing to use their non-violent power for good, will help them to recognize there is no security in avoiding or not bringing into being the things of most value to life, such as Peace and an equal fairness that creates good will among people.

Find your friends among Golden Rule like groups, to be able to network with others locally, nationally, and world wide, so that many can be aware and decide on the best ways to help, and work together towards mutual needs and actions, when and where progress can be most beneficial.

Start mornings with gratitude, even for the breath of another day, and pray for a better day by asking The Holy Spirit to guide you where you could best be, or where your help will be most needed. Be assured that what ever you give with a Loving Heart, will be returned to you 100 fold, in this life as well as in the next, Jesus promised such an increase to those who would "hear"!

In one form or another I have found this to be true, but usually it can only be seen in retrospect, for in the process of giving, it is better to not think of it's cost or you'll tend to lean towards self-pity when you can see no immediate reward.

Jesus assures us in the writings of the Disciple John, that those who would "hear my word, and believe on God, 'ABBA' who sent me, have everlasting life and shall not come into condemnation but have passed from death unto life." John 5:24

For those who doubt an everlasting life after this one, consider that even if there were nothing, you would still have, while living here, the satisfaction of knowing you are doing your best, with your best! That is an instant living reward in itself, and the opposite is a terrible feeling to live with, when you realize the harm you may have caused or be causing others or yourself!

DESMOND TUTU SPEAKS

"People of religion have no choice in the matter.

Where there is injustice and oppression, where people are treated as if they were less than who they are-those created in the image of God- you have no choice but to oppose...that injustice and oppression."

"We do our religions scant justice, we put our religions into disrepute, if we do not stand up for the truth, if we do not stand up for justice, if we are not the voice of the voiceless ones, if we are not those who stand up for those who cannot stand up for themselves."

"Ubuntu" is the African word for the essence of being human. It speaks of how my humanity is caught up and bound up inextricably with yours.

We are made for togetherness, for family, interdependence with our fellow human beings, with the rest of creation."

"We inhabit a universe that is characterized by diversity.

There is room for everyone; there is room for every culture, race, language, and point of view."

"Almost everywhere the rulers are out of touch with the people."

FORMING EVOLUTIONARY RELATIONSHIPS

Can we really be alone here on this little planet, in a huge and expanding universe? Can this be an evolutionary trial and error maze, the survival of the physical or moral fittest, or for those best able to be adaptable?

Could there be life on other planets, some more advanced than we, who may have already come here to visit, to help, just as we seek to explore outer space, or could some even be here to take advantage of us?

Possible yes to all these potentials, but we have little evidence that we can scientifically prove, like being in a laboratory repeatable, or we can say are beyond doubt either way, at this point.

Yet anyone who has seen a clear night view of the uncountable numbers of stars similar to our own sun, can hardly help but wonder about the possibilities in the now known billions of planets around other suns, and must find it hard to believe there could not be numerous kinds of living beings out there in our mostly yet unknown and unexplored vast Universe.

Think of all the numerous varieties of life here, just on our little planet. The potentials and probabilities are undeniable. Nor can life be limited to just what can be seen within our own physical matter, based on carbon atoms.

We best not limit! For there is evidence of the existence of hard to explain things like electricity, zillions of life under a microscopic, x-rays, gamma rays, we see and know only a small range, beyond our physical eyes limited sight.

There are many evidences of what we call extra ordinary Spiritual experiences but they cannot be physically repeated as required for a physical scientific study.

When one has a personal encounter with what they believe is spiritual, it can best be judged as to whether it is harmful or helpful to the person, to the whole, for the common good. Spiritual encounters from God are given primarily for the common good!

Negative encounters from a negative spiritual source would be for more selfish purposes and reasons, to frighten, to control, even to gain entrance to the soul, to take over one's free will. Better off avoiding as many negative encounters as possible.

People who have never experienced any kind of a spiritual encounter may be naturally doubtful of the reality of either negative or positive spirits.

Some have been sincere in asking for a sign, often at a great point of need in their life wanting very badly some miraculous sign or certainty, and when not receiving such a sign they then usually conclude there is no God!

I did that once in my late teens and felt deserted when there was no response. No help I felt I needed at that time and so decided God must be dead or in another part of the universe.

It would be nine years later before I would not just ask for a sign from God but be willing to give my all, in first repentance for two weeks, before I finally received an answer.

Few humans have had much control over what has been best for us to know at any specific time, and trying to conjure up any kind of a Spirit for answers is asking for trouble.

Better to seek the "faith of a mustard seed" with patience, that what you need to know will be known in God's time.

Signs are not normally given by demand. I tend to think from what I've learned, only in specific circumstances where a cosmic intervention is indicated are miraculous signs given at all.

Contrary to some religious teachings sooner or later most of us experience that "the rain as well as the sun falls on the good as well as the bad", and God is "not a god of partiality". *Duet.10:18; Act:10:34; Romans 2:11

Many tend to lose their faith when bad things happen to good people. They feel if there had been a God they would have been protected from any harm.

I have known that feeling well. I also have known what it is like to have miraculous things happen but never for a special favor for me alone, only for the benefit of the whole.

There is a negative force you can bargain with for favors but like Casino's they are there to take your money, so to speak or whatever you have that is most valuable to a negative one, like your soul.

Without any unseen faith or hope, we find ourselves living mostly in a physical "shell" where we will feel spiritually alone, then we tend to look for human comfort, but that can only be a temporary fix. God is what fills the eternal need for wholeness in our soul.

To have that hope, is better than to have none! Especially when it comes to the mysteries of Spiritual knowledge, that is in God's best time to share and not ours.

Faith can be an act of power in itself, for either good or evil, so it is equally important just what it is, that you are putting your faith in! A lack of certainty works both ways in doubting but ultimately some degree of just plain holding on to faith or hope, even when there is no answer, is needed.

There are chemicals and electrical brain stimulations that are capable of producing out of the normal, extra-ordinary experiences by opening up the gates of the spiritual world but such shortcuts are rarely recommended, as they pose personal psychological dangers.

Such as playing with an Ouija board, or just by thinking too many negative thoughts, lots of things can be opening up a pathway to a negative spirit, or experiences you may later regret having caused.

The fruits of experience with the spiritual world for anyone, must be judged to be good or bad not just for the individual, but equally as well, for the whole? This may or may not be judged in one generation correctly, often in the past it has not been.

Our faith tends to grow with time and experience, or it will tend to shrink into little or even nothing at all, when we shy away from a Godly experience or any feeling of closeness with A Divine and unconditional Love.

"No one can see God"?

Maybe what is really meant is we see only in part, and according to our physical minds spiritual limitations. Not being able to see the fullness of God is perhaps why so many paintings and other forms of art are usually set in the cultural times they were created in, with clothes and facial features of that artist time. In our patriarchal times most often in masculine forms, described by masculine terms.

Down through our knowable history people have reported to see what they believed to be visitors from "The Skies", some even claiming to be from other planets.

There are ancient paintings and statues that resembling space outfits we now use in our own times, needed to go out into space safely.

Ancient writings, as in India, tell of advanced civilizations being destroyed by means of advanced destruction even for our own day. Usually seemingly because of their leaders excessive greed for power and war, much like we face in our world now.

In the past there may have been many civilizations, who became too greedy, uncaring, and seemed to cause their own destruction, as much of our world seems now on the verge of doing?

Yet many of our ways, or traditions, have evolved over time for the better, such as slavery, racism and sexism, and other forms of inequality. We've come a long way in making them better! Those less evolved or caught up in forms of addictive greed and power tripping, have continued in the misuse of many people. We will need many working together to be able to stop their misusing of more, potentially most, already now in many ways.

We seem to have a natural tendency to shy away from complex or difficult situations, as we shy away from people who don't see things the way we do, yet if we want to grow in wisdom and truth, we have to do our best to listen as intuitively as we can, not just with our human logic that is limited but to seek and abide by Universal Truths of acting in Good Will for all.

This can be fearful, the feeling of not wanting to get involved, or not overwhelmed before even trying! To do what we can to change what we may have unconsciously been impressed with, since early childhood, such as inequality, inferiority or superiority.

Yet in our present circumstances that is involving life and death decisions for millions even billions of people, we each have a need to consider a radical change in our attitudes towards our present ingrained sense of inequality.

I really "see" the world's consciousness trying to make that leap and I want to believe that enough do realize the need but I also see the Powers that be, like the Pharaohs of old, refusing to budge.

In the Scriptures of the Bible, over 200 times God's Hand is mentioned, each time during a point when God has decided to intervene through his people.

The year that I saw God's Hand was about the time of the first invasion of WW II 1939, after Germany made Hitler their President. I believe now to try to prevent an even worse World War III in our times, without taking away our free will?

I have not literally seen that Hand again but did physically feel it one more time, it's obvious felt power then and later was by far the most powerful thing I have ever felt.

For God is the most powerful Being, a living God who invites you right now to live life eternally too!

It takes at least "empathy" to live a good life, but it may also take knowing that you have asked God's Spirit to live within you, for a more positive assurance of eternal life.

The Word of Prophecy "Equality" came from God at my Spiritual "Rebirth", when I was about 29 years old. Intellectually I had had my doubts since college, even of God's existence or at least any concern with our 'puny' lives as I was seeing us as but a speck in our huge Milky Way of stars.

Yet in remembering the seeing of God's Hand at five years old I felt I had to know for sure, one way or the other so I asked for a Biblical "Fleece", by fasting and praying for two weeks as much as I could while I continued to work.

At the end on a Sunday I sat down in my living room in a favorite easy chair, my children gone with their Father to visit their Grandparents. I said to myself: "Well, I cannot fast or pray anymore, I guess there is no God or surely I would have had a sign by now".

Immediately through the walls of the room I felt God's Spirit, not only fill up the room but also fully wash over me and I heard clearly the one distinct word of "EQUALITY".

Since then realizing this was to be my mission in life, I have studied as much as I could the meaning of this word and it's many analogies such as "God is not a god of partiality". Many similar scriptural words such as "God is not a respecter of persons", God does not have favorites, God's Equity, Equal Justice, Mercy!

Also have tried my best to live it.

It can sure seem like God has favorites. Such as when we win over someone else's efforts we can feel God is with us and not with the other side, and that has been expressed in all scriptures by the side writing them, just as when we lose, we tend to think God is not with us.

Have learned God is here with all of us, all the time.

We make the choice, consciously or unconsciously, to walk away by our free will, or we may just naturally separate ourselves from not wanting to feel the Holiness of God, when what we are doing we think or know, is not good and it is in our own separating that we feel the loss of God within us.

Sometimes we are influenced by others or allow them to separate us from feeling God's presence. Sometimes because things don't go fairly for us we even blame God instead of the situation we happen to be in, by choice or accident.

In the sharing of this life it is our responsibility, as well as others, to be Loving and Fair, to help create a Loving and fair or Just life for others, as well as our self.

Those who are not able to care, need the help of the whole community. We will need to find cures for our emotional and mental ills as much as we need to seek cures for all ills!

I know from knowing a God of Holy Love that each one of us are considered a special unique creation, ever growing spiritually if we are trying at all; all the time being equally loved by God. Praise God for that kind of Holy Love.

Thank God for our Equal Human Rights, for the Freedom that stops only at the rights of another.

What Jesus said, summed up the Laws and the Prophets to Love One Another, similar to the Universal Golden Rule even found in the hearts of non-believers, found in all those who have not become bitter or damaged from life.

A Universal Golden Rule does not justify inequality for females, or low unjust wages that now force so many of our world's people on a starvation diet and dire poverty.

Nor the thousands of children who actually starve to death every day, while millions more go to bed hungry every night. Children not being able to go to school because they must go to work at 5-6 years old!

This is my witnessing as the most needed priority for our times! It is something you should be able to confirm for yourself, if you have or want your own loving relationship with a: "God who is Love, and when we love, we live in God, and God lives in us." * * I John 4:16.

Many of our relationships I've found, are based on "I'll comfort you, if you'll comfort me" and much in-between. To go beyond a fragile comfort zone, we need to purposely try to build relationships with the aim of helping each other to grow evolutionary wise?

Maybe because we need that stretching of our minds sight, to see beyond our own ego's comfort, as our world has so many desperately needs right now.

What are some ways we could do that? One of the best ways I've found is not to take offense at what others say. Not to immediately take offense personally takes will power.

Anything that seems a put down is maybe being said to help you grow, but usually it is just from someone's grumpy mood, or his or her ego problem, in some stage of inequality.

It is all very contagious so that is why you want to back away and don't let it affect you personally.

To form evolutionary relationships with others means being aware of the possible whys for their negative actions, that is usually from some form of inequality, fears, envy, limiting beliefs, or imposing not so good traditions from the past.

These can keep us from being objective, calm and collected, to act in the best non-violent way to deal with our own or others negative actions.

Some seeking positive change believe a most immediate or the fastest balance of political power and economic fairness could be achieved through democratically controlled, equally owned People's Co-Operatives, instead of those run only for the profit of a few.

More pooling of peoples needs and resources should be considered in our efforts at creating a more Cooperative World.

Cooperative Golden Rule groups could be a good place to begin in your own individual communities, depending on your interest, resources, time, and energy.

Many I've known who seem able to accept our need to end inequality also seem to be good people who are doing their best to treat others with equal fairness.

Many believe in the Gospels, to "Love God and Love One Another", or have beliefs that include the Universal Golden Rule.

At the other extreme, there are also those who seem so cold, believe in our present day inequality, and seem incapable of hearing, believing, or accepting any growth into "Equality"!

People can be nicely dressed and polished on the surface, but what is inside, or their true motives, are not so easy to recognize, some being masters of deception, unless you are directly affected by their actions or have personally experience their cruelty and selfishness, by their words and actions towards those they have power over.

When you look at our world and see the mess it is in, you realize there may be many people in power, with little or no compassion, empathy, or love for others or at the most care only about those who are most like themselves.

It may be on an unconscious level or a conscious level or even where a spirit of evil is really their master.

Am also realizing my trying to appeal to the better side of some is not working, because one way or another they have already decided or sold out to a spirit that doesn't want to change, to be any better or what they see as different. In all of us there is this big reluctance to change, even sometimes for the better!

A false Image of God may be at the root of justifying many wrong actions. It is for a very good reason against the first of the Biblical Ten Commandments, to not make a "graven Image", a material, or a human Image of God.

God is Spirit, and we are too but are mostly in a fleshly worldly state and while here on this earth we are tied to a physical body that is weak, no matter how strong we appear to be.

By not allowing women to be Ordained, and the continued use of the patriarchal language, the Church has been one of the biggest promoters of this false male Image of God, or "Idolatry".

So while I feel it is right to concentrate on the members of my Church, I also know many of those who are left within it, are those who have been the most indoctrinated.

Change within religions need to come from the top down too, as representing a God who is Equally for All.

Hopefully the new survey Pope Francis sent out will get to enough of those, who do try to follow God's Will rather than man's, and will be more evidence he needs to act with.

I will have to wait and see for he has set a timetable for this next year of 2015, am going to keep my hopes high, for he seems like such a holy one. When I finally finish writing as best I can, will send him the final more complete copy as I have already sent a preliminary one.

Some I pray will feel led to also share their views to end discrimination and inequality. He has many secretaries to keep him informed of what he receives by mail at the Vatican in Rome from the people. One can also Tweet Pope Francis. The Has-tag is @Pontiff

There seems nothing more for me to say but pray you will do your best to create your own Golden Rule groups, to network with others at sites such as:

www.worldwidehumanrights.org

Have written this message of Equal Rights From God to be easily shared at a low price for paperback book, and just $1 as e-book, at www.Amazon.com. To be one of many ways to network with others.

May God's Peace Be with you in all the good things you do. IThes. 5:15...

Made in the USA
Columbia, SC
22 May 2023

16671458R00085